The Mini **Rough Guide** to
RIGA

T0343662

YOUR TAILOR-MADE TRIP STARTS HERE

Tailor-made trips and unique adventures crafted by local experts

HOW ROUGHGUIDES.COM/TRIPS WORKS

STEP 1

Pick your dream destination, tell us what you want and submit an enquiry.

STEP 2

Fill in a short form to tell your local expert about you dream trip and preference

STEP 3

Our local expert will craft your tailor-made itinerary. You'll be able to tweak and refine it until you're completely satisfied.

STEP 4

Book online with ease, pac your bags and enjoy the trip! Our local expert will b on hand 24/7 while you're on the road.

PLAN AND BOOK YOUR TRIP AT
ROUGHGUIDES.COM/TRIPS

How to download your Free eBook

1. Visit **www.roughguides.com/free-ebook** or scan the **QR code** opposite

2. Enter the code **riga955**

3. Follow the simple step-by-step instructions

For troubleshooting contact: mail@roughguides.com

Contents

Introduction

The largest city in the Baltics, Riga is also one of its most exciting. Located near the mouth of the River Daugava on the Baltic Sea, it is endowed with the beautiful gabled homes and storehouses built by medieval merchants. Gothic church spires pierce the skyline, and an imposing crusader castle stands sentinel over the city. Then there's the abundance of Art Nouveau riches – nearly one-third of the city's buildings – many designed by architect Mikhail Eisenstein, father of the Riga-born filmmaker Sergei Eisenstein. Riga's contemporary face plays out in its cultural and arts venues,

WHAT'S NEW

Plans are underway on the design of Riga's brand-new concert hall, slated to open by 2030, for which foundations were laid on a dam on the River Daugava back in 2010. Another new face making waves on the cultural scene, the Museum of Contemporary Art (www.lmocaf.org) is set in a former power plant in Riga's port. Designed by Rem Koolhaas, the gallery space was due to open in 2021 but has sputtered to a halt due to funding issues; watch this space. Restored in 2022, Āgenskalns tirgus (Nometņu iela 64) – Riga's oldest market – is now a tempting foodie enclave with a cluster of small, independent speciality shops selling aromatic spices, artisan ice cream and locally roasted coffee. On the first floor, there's a food hall serving the likes of wood-fired pizzas, borscht (beetroot soup) and *khinkali* (Georgian dumplings). The former Moscow District (Maskavas forštate), which initially took its name because the main road to the Russian capital ran through it, was renamed as the Latgale neighbourhood (Latgales apkaime) in 2024, though is still referred to colloquially by that moniker. Long a cool enclave with a rebellious streak, the warehouse quarter (also known as Spīķeri), has become a trendy hangout full of cafés, bars, clubs and art galleries housed in renovated yellow-brick buildings.

The fine Art Nouveau streets of Riga

inventive bars and Michelin-recognised restaurants. The Latvian capital's thriving food scene sees a growing crop of innovative restaurants spring up between bierkellers and old inns. Beyond its historic core are the manicured parks and tree-lined boulevards of the New Town, while nearby is locals' favourite summer hangout, the breezy coastal resort of Jūrmala. Yet, despite this, Riga remains gloriously under the radar, free from the crowds that plague the likes of Prague or Budapest.

A COSMOPOLITAN CITY

From its medieval golden age as the largest city in the Swedish Empire to its early-twentieth-century heyday as an economic powerhouse and Russia's third-largest port, Riga has long been a symbol of cosmopolitan living.

WHEN TO VISIT

Riga's climate is continental, with a short but relatively mild summer when average temperatures hover around 17°C, and days are long and bright. That said, the season is also notable for occasional heavy rainfall, so pack a raincoat as well as an umbrella. Although the city is becoming increasingly popular, it's not difficult to find accommodation at short notice, even in July and August. Winters are often wet, with very little sunlight to lift the gloom. From November, it turns much colder and damper, and there can be substantial snowfall; in fact, it's not uncommon for Riga to experience snow flurries as late as April. January and February are particularly biting, even reaching -30°C on the coldest days. Nevertheless, Riga looks magical in the snow, and one of the joys is being able to warm up in one of the city's cosy cafés or pubs. A good month to visit Riga is October, when temperatures haven't yet plummeted, the weather remains pleasant enough for outdoor strolls and most places are still open. From March onwards, Riga begins to brighten up, the days get longer, and the mercury begins to creep northwards. However, you'd still do well to pack warm clothing, plus waterproof coats and boots.

During the Cold War, Latvia's only major metropolis languished behind the Iron Curtain. Despite sustaining oppression under Soviet rule, Latvia quietly resisted cultural conformity.

Though the various occupiers through the years have left their mark on the city's food, architecture, culture and language, the residents of Riga remain fiercely independent and fiercely proud, holding on tightly to ancient Latvian traditions and beliefs but always looking to the future.

OLD MEETS NEW

Riga sprawls across an area of three hundred square kilometres (115 sq miles) and is home to over a third of Latvia's 1.95 million inhabitants. The city is divided by the yawning River Daugava, and most of the historical sights are strung along the right bank around the UNESCO-listed old town, or *Vecriga*. Here you will find Dutch Renaissance apartment houses, thirteenth-century churches and picturesque squares that can compete with the finest Europe has to offer.

Venture beyond its cobblestoned core and you'll discover a modern, cosmopolitan city with busy boulevards, nineteenth-century parks, and the most concentrated collection of Art Nouveau buildings found anywhere on the European continent. And journey just half an hour outside the city and you can explore acres of untouched forest or stretches of sandy beach.

Best of all, Riga exudes a big-city feel without actually being one. In fact, most of its attractions can be reached on foot or by a short tram ride.

Scenic canal rides through Riga

CULTURAL RICHES

Folklore and legend may underpin many of ancient Latvian traditions, but it's this rich cultural inheritance that makes its music and arts so forceful today. Artists no longer need national myths to sustain them, a new generation of forward-thinking creatives are pushing the agenda. There are theatre performances, festivals, art exhibitions and concerts galore in Riga, and its National Opera and Ballet is the most dynamic

⌐ SUSTAINABLE TRAVEL

Sustainable cuisine showcasing the bounty of the land is the new hallmark of contemporary Latvian cooking. It's a trend that stretches from the homely fare dished up in unpretentious inns to innovative plates served in culinary big-hitters, such as the Michelin-starred *Max Cekot Kitchen*. Buying produce from food markets like Āgenskalns tirgus or Central Market instead of supermarkets offers visitors the opportunity to pick up local cheeses, charcuterie, honeys, jams and preserves brought into town from outlying farms. The typically Baltic high-tech approach to modern life is frequently applied to concerns about the environment and sustainability. If you need to visit places that are not easily accessible via public transport, a variety of useful car-sharing apps have been developed to keep people mobile while reducing the number of private vehicles on the roads. Try CityBee (https://citybee.lt). And for those planning to venture further afield beyond Latvia, it will become a lot easier when Rail Baltica, the much-vaunted high-speed rail link set to connect the Baltic capitals, starts up around 2030. This will open up travel between Estonia, Lithuania and Latvia even further, and make slow and sustainable travel a breeze.

in the Baltic States. The country has long spawned top-drawer talent like playwright Jānis Pliekšāns and artists Vilhelms Purvītis, Janīs Rozentāls and Jānis Valters. Latvia is also famous for producing world-renowned opera singers and ballet dancers, including Mikhail Baryshnikov.

Writers like Vizma Belševica and Knuts Skujenieks were censored and repressed during the Soviet era but channeled this stifled creativity into producing world-acclaimed art.

The opening of the landmark National Library in 2014 was a symbol of Latvia's cultural renaissance, and there are further plans in the pipeline to open a Museum of Contemporary Art and new concert hall.

CUISINE AND CRAFT BEER

Latvia's chefs too are reconnecting with traditional Latvian culture through food. Michelin published its internationally acclaimed list of recommended restaurants in Latvia in 2023; *Max Cekot Kitchen* in Riga was the country's first restaurant to be awarded a Michelin star. Whether you're dining in a top culinary postcode or an unassuming inn, you'll discover the new hallmark of modern Baltic cooking is sustainable cuisine featuring fresh, seasonal, locally sourced ingredients. The best place to discover the natural larder of Latvia is in its huge Central Market, spread across a series of Zeppelin hangars; each dedicated to a speciality: meat, dairy produce, vegetables and seafood. Here, cream is sold in plastic bags, there are barrels of sauerkraut, fancy cakes, pickled garlic, mounds of dried herbs and mushrooms, smoked fish and whole stalls selling nothing but tins of sardines.

Āgenskalns tirgus

Craft beer is far from being a modern trend in Latvia; it's a deeply embedded aspect of local culture. Yet a recent renaissance sees bars across the capital act as a showcase for small-scale producers. Valmiermuiža in Riga not only produces its own unique brews but also uses solar-panel energy to power its vats – just one of the growing crop of Latvian companies embodying the experimental spirit of the innovative vanguard.

10 Things not to miss

A perfect day in Riga

9AM

Central Market. Start the day with a visit to the Central Market (see page 72). Wander through the series of huge Zeppelin hangars, each with its own speciality: fish, dairy, fruit and vegetables, and meat.

10AM

Culture trail. Take a walk through the Latgale neighbourhood, located behind the market, with its nineteenth-century wooden houses and warehouse quarter (Spiķeri) full of trendy cafés, bars, clubs and art galleries. If you fancy a museum, there is the small Riga Ghetto and Latvian Holocaust Museum (see page 73) that commemorates the victims of the Holocaust.

11AM

Old Riga. Head for the old town to visit the excellent Museum of the Occupation of Latvia, which recounts Latvia's painful history. Afterwards, take a walk around the cobblestone streets of Riga's medieval core. Don't miss Sts Peter and Paul Church and the Dome Cathedral (see page 47).

12.30PM

Lunch. The table to book is at the elegant *Melnie Mūki* restaurant (see page 118), tucked inside a section of a medieval convent. Check out the chef's specials, which usually include a classic Latvian dish, best washed down with a locally brewed beer.

2PM

Art Nouveau wonders. Head to the Art Nouveau district (see page 69) to discover one of the most beautiful corners of the capital. The flamboyant architectural style became a symbol of Riga's golden age when, at the end of the nineteenth century, the city's wealth was at its zenith.

5PM

Shopping. Explore the pleasant parks that form a green strip near the city centre; don't miss the Freedom Monument and Laima Clock (see page 62). For shopping, head to trendy Bergs Bazaar (see page 65) to buy handmade chocolates, fragrant soaps and local linens.

8PM

Dinner. Round up the day at *Milda* (see page 118), whose name nods to the figure atop the Freedom Monument. It might look unassuming from the outside, but its menu is anything but. In fact, its modern twist on Latvian classics has earned the restaurant a bib gourmand in Latvia's inaugural Michelin guide.

10.30PM

A night on the town. Start in *Gimlet*, a cool bar serving cocktails infused with Nordic herbs (see page 95), then see what's happening at local cultural hub Kaņepes Kultūras centrs (see page 94), before heading to *Cloud Nine* for dancing to live DJ sets (see page 95).

Art Nouveau Riga

9AM

Alberta iela. The best place to start an Art Nouveau tour of Riga is on Albert Street, where most of the houses on the right side (plus No. 13 opposite) were designed by Mikhail Eisenstein, father of filmmaker Sergei Eisenstein, the director behind the 1925 epic *Battleship Potemkin*. Next, duck down Strēlnieku iela to see another of Eisenstein's masterpieces at No. 4a, adorned with his characteristic bright blue touch.

11AM

Riga Art Nouveau Museum. The house that the Latvian architect Konstantins Pēkšēns built for himself has now been converted into a museum (see page 71). The seven ground-floor rooms, including bathroom and kitchen, are all fitted with Art Nouveau fixtures and furniture.

NOON

Rozentāls and Blaumanis Museum. This top-floor house-museum is designed to look as it would have when two of its most famous residents lived here: artist Janis Rozentāls (1866–1916) and writer Rūdolfs Blaumanis (1863–1908). Walls are hung with Rozentāls' paintings of early-twentieth-century Riga, his family and friends. See page 71.

1PM

Elizabetes iela. On this street you'll find some of the finest works by Riga's architectural poster child, Eisenstein: No. 33, which looks like a frothy wedding cake; No. 10b, with the incredibly long human faces either side of a peacock; and No. 10a, with its hints of Biological Romanticism.

2.30PM

Latvian Academy of Arts. Walk through Esplanāde Park to the former Stock Exchange, built by one of Riga's most important architects, the Baltic German Wilhelm Bockslaff, in 1905. Since 1919 the graceful building has housed the Latvian Academy of Arts, whose ceiling, embroidered after the style of William Morris, is a treasury of stained glass. See page 69.

3.30PM

The Three Brothers. These dollhouse-dinky fifteenth-century merchants' homes are the oldest residences in the city. Inside shows how the families would have lived on the lower floors while leaving the upper areas free for storage. One is home to the interesting Latvian Architecture Museum (www.archmuseum.lv). See page 53.

4PM

Smilšu iela. One of the city's oldest streets, Smilšu is littered with early-twentieth-century architecture. No. 2, built in 1902, is an exemplification of Biological Romanticism. Its facade is adorned with a huge peacock, trees and humans with roots in place of legs. No. 8 is a riot of gargoyles and cherubs; peek inside the foyer to see the elaborate floral designs.

Outdoor Riga

9AM

Kronvalda Park. Take an early-morning stroll through the canal-threaded park, named after Atis Kronvalds (1837–75), the Latvian linguist and teacher who later came to symbolise the National Awakening. Near the World Trade Centre, formerly the home of the Central Committee of the Communist Party of Latvia, look out for the fragment of the Berlin Wall on display, donated to the city by the museum at Checkpoint Charlie. See page 60.

11AM

Freedom Monument. Make your way to the Freedom Monument, referred to endearingly by locals as Milda, where a statue of Mother Latvia holds three golden stars representing the historic regions of the country: Kurzeme, Vidzeme and Latgale. See page 62.

11.30AM

National Opera House. Stroll to the opulent National Opera House, a symbol of Latvian pride. Now home to the Riga opera and ballet companies, its stage was once graced by native sons Mikhail Baryshnikov and Boris Gudunov. Outside, manicured gardens are arranged around a fine fountain. See page 63.

NOON

Lunch. Head to the beautiful Vērmane Park, whose leafy gardens wrap around *Whitehouse*, one of Riga's finest restaurants. Here, chefs give a contemporary spin to Latvian classics, all served with a side of lush green views through floor-length windows. See page 121.

1.30PM

Wöhrmann Park. Wander through one of Riga's oldest parks, a favourite locals' hangout where pensioners play chess in the restored amphitheatre in the summer. See page 65.

2PM

Esplanāde Park. Press on to the Esplanāde (see page 67), a luscious park that hosts cultural events and fairs, including Riga's 700th anniversary celebrations in 1901. Here you will find the 1884-built Russian Orthodox Cathedral, whose five gilded cupolas and adjoining belfry was intended to symbolise the power of the 'true faith' in the Baltics in an era when all other languages other than Russian were suppressed.

3PM

Ethnographic Open-Air Museum of Latvia. Take bus No. 1 from Tērbatas to the Ethnographic Open-Air Museum of Latvia, which reveals a slice of nineteenth-century Latvia. Founded in 1924, this sprawling recreated village of typical wooden homes, shops, churches and windmills today shows weavers, blacksmiths, beekeepers and various craftspeople going about their business as they have for years. You can easily pass an afternoon here. See page 80.

History

Riga's history is complex, but much of it can be explained by the city's chief purpose as the focal point of commerce in the region. Since its founding in 1201, the port city has been coveted by all of its neighbouring powers. Its prime location at the mouth of the River Daugava on the Baltic Sea ensured its status as a window on the vast resources of the Russian lands in the east, and its natural harbour guaranteed a constant flow of luxury goods from the west. This has been the key to its prosperity and also its curse.

On the eve of Riga's founding, four tribal kingdoms coexisted on the territory that is now Latvia. These ancient ancestors of the Latvians led a sedentary life and spoke a Baltic language similar to that used by Lithuanian and Prussian tribes to the south. A fifth group of inhabitants called the Livs had settled in small fishing villages along the coastline and spoke a Finno-Ugric language closely related to that spoken by present-day Estonians. For centuries, these groups lived and fought among one another on these shores, often trading amber, honey and animal skins with far-flung cultures around Europe and even the Middle East. Tacitus and Herodotus both mention the amber routes of antiquity and their origin in the Baltic lands.

THE NORTHERN CRUSADE

By the twelfth century, the raids of barbarous Vikings were no longer a threat, but a new foe surfaced, disguised as messengers of Christ. German traders began arriving at the mouth of the River Daugava in the 1100s and took back to their native cities stories of the prosperous lands in the north populated by pagan savages. Before long, merchants and priests arrived in droves, but it wasn't until Bishop Albert von Buxhoevden from Bremen obtained a papal bull to begin a church-sanctioned crusade against the infidels that the real trouble began.

Albert did not want to repeat the mistake of his predecessor, Bishop Berthold of Hanover, who was stabbed with a spear and literally torn to pieces by the Livs. Upon his arrival in 1201, Albert began construction of a fortress to protect himself and his men, and this year is widely accepted as the official date of the founding of Riga. Facing opposition by volatile local tribes, Albert created the Livonian Order the following year, which is also known as the Order of the Brotherhood of the Sword.

In the coming decades Riga was a frequent target of raiding parties by indigenous tribes, but because of its excellent fortifications the city was never taken. The Order continued to conquer the lands of the four Latvian tribes – the Cours, Semigallians, Selonians and Letts – often pitting one against the other. The tribes lacked

Riga and the River Daugava, a copperplate engraving from 1638

HANSEATIC LEAGUE

Riga's wealth in the late Middle Ages was in part due to its joining in 1282 of the Hanseatic League, Europe's first free-trade organisation. The league was started by German merchant societies (Hanse) to protect the herring trade in Lübeck and its vital salt suppliers in Hamburg. The alliance soon developed into a powerful confederation of more than 150 port-cities that came to control the shipping of fish, flax, fur, grain, honey and timber from Russia and the Baltics, and cloth and other goods manufactured by Flemish and English guilds. Riga had exclusive rights to transport goods along the River Daugava, and Livonia had its own Hanseatic diet or parliament. The Hansa merchants left their mark on the towns and cities where they were established and much of Old Riga is characterised by the red-brick, step-gabled buildings common to Hansa ports.

unity and began to fall one by one until they were all subjugated, by 1290. The Order, however, was no match for the neighbouring Lithuanians, who inflicted devastating defeats upon them in 1236 and 1260 with the help of rebellious Latvian tribes.

The next two centuries were marked by the increasing prosperity of Riga, and the ceaseless struggle for power between the Bishop of Riga, the town council and the Order. The hated Order gained the upper hand due to its size and military strength, but its forays into the Russian lands to the east met with disaster at the hands of Alexander Nevski at Lake Peipus. In 1410 at the Battle of Tannenberg, overwhelming Polish and Lithuanian forces decisively beat the Teutonic Order, to which the Livonian Order also belonged. More crusaders were eventually assembled and the Livonian Order once again conquered Riga in 1491.

POLES AND SWEDES

Martin Luther's Reformation arrived in Riga in 1522 and was widely embraced by the populace. The bishop of Riga lost his credibility and the town council became the most powerful force in local politics. The old Order no longer served much purpose, as most of its knights had become wealthy landowners. Increasing Russian raids from the east caused the last grand master of the Order to swear his allegiance to the Polish king in 1561.

In return, the grand master was given land in western Livonia, which became the Duchy of Courland. The Livonian Order ceased to exist, but Riga was forced to accept Polish rule and the unpopular Catholic faith.

In 1600, war erupted between Poland and Sweden and by 1621, Gustavus Adolphus's forces had laid siege to Riga. The city eventually surrendered to the Swedish king and a new era of learning, public works and increased trade began. Schools and hospitals were built across Swedish Livonia, the first newspaper was published, the first code of laws was implemented and the Bible was translated into Latvian. Russian troops attacked the city in 1656, but despite overwhelming odds, the city's defenders thwarted the Russians' efforts, forcing them to retreat. Relative peace ruled the realm for roughly another half century. At this time, Riga was the largest city in the Swedish Empire, which included much of present-day Scandinavia, Latvia, Estonia and parts of Poland and Germany.

House of Blackheads

THE RUSSIAN EMPIRE

By 1700, the Russian Empire was expanding and it desperately wanted a foothold on the Baltic Sea, which was completely dominated by the Kingdom of Sweden. The Great Northern War between the two powers would engulf the region for more than 20 years, laying waste to the once prosperous lands of what is now Latvia. Less than 100,000 inhabitants of Livonia would survive the carnage and the ensuing plague.

In the middle of the night on 6 April 1709, an omen of terrible things to come awoke the citizens of Riga. A huge ice sheet broke free in the river causing a major flood that left much of the city under water. By October, Russian forces had reached the gates of the city. After seven months of siege and fierce canon bombardment, Riga surrendered to the armies of Peter the Great in June 1710. By the end of the century all of Livonia had been conquered by Russia. In Riga, the Germans of the town council and the guilds began excluding Latvians from all positions of power, while the land barons gained complete control of their Latvian serfs, abusing and torturing them at will and in some cases even selling and trading them as slaves.

NOTES

In the 1640s, Duke Jacob of Courland (1610–82) owned colonies in Gambia, Africa, and the island of Tobago in the Caribbean. He presided over a vast maritime fleet and was considered to be one of the wealthiest Europeans of his day. Today, Tobago's Great Courland Bay is a testament to its short-lived colonisation by Latvians and Baltic Germans.

THE LATVIAN AWAKENING

The nineteenth century brought both hardship and prosperity to Riga. Believing Napoleon's troops were headed for the city, a hasty decision was made by local Russian commanders to raze the wooden buildings of the suburbs. A small contingent

Town Hall Square, oil on canvas by K.T. Sechhelm (1819)

of Napoleon's forces did eventually reach Riga, but the majority of his army headed directly for Moscow, instead of via the Baltics to St Petersburg, as many had feared. Riga was never taken.

Despite the abolition of serfdom in Latvia, peasant revolts erupted in the countryside for two years from 1817. Former serfs were no longer obliged to work the land, but they had nowhere to go and were forbidden from owning property, which effectively worsened their lot. By the second half of the century a national awakening began as intellectuals started educating the masses about their rights. The first Latvian newspapers were published, and the first Latvian Song Festival was held in 1873. Meanwhile, the city experienced a boom time, and it grew to become the third-largest port city in the Russian Empire. The archaic prohibition against constructing stone buildings outside the city walls

Midsummer's Eve Festival, a lithograph by T.H. Rickmann (1842)

was lifted and the ancient walls and ramparts were torn down. It was during this period of unprecedented wealth and expansion that much of the city took on its current appearance.

THE TWENTIETH CENTURY

In 1901 the city celebrated its 700th anniversary with much fanfare, but only four years later revolution overwhelmed Riga. Fifty thousand demonstrators took to the streets, provoking a brutal crackdown on striking factory workers. The tsar granted concessions, but also sent 'punishment brigades' to the region which executed nearly two thousand Latvians.

World War I brought both pain and opportunity. By 1915, half of Latvian territory was occupied by German forces and Russia allowed Latvians to raise an army to defend the country from invaders. On 18 November 1918, just seven days after Germany surrendered, a congress of Latvian intellectuals seized the opportunity and declared Latvia's independence. But the euphoria was short-lived and by 1919, Riga was captured by Russian Red forces. With renegade German troops, the Latvians repelled the communists, but then fought one another for control of the country. The Germans were eventually defeated and the Soviet Union signed a peace treaty in 1921 and withdrew its forces.

Although the country was devastated by yet another war, the economy quickly rebounded and, by the 1930s, Latvia enjoyed one of the highest standards of living in Europe. Frustrated with the incessant squabbles of parliamentarians, one of Latvia's founding fathers, Kārlis Ulmanis, staged a bloodless coup in 1934 and set up a dictatorship. Democracy hadn't lasted long, but the new regime would only survive another six years. Larger forces were at play.

In 1939 Nazi Germany and the Soviet Union signed the Molotov–Ribbentrop pact, which divided Eastern Europe into German and Soviet spheres of influence. Given an ultimatum by the Soviets to allow its army to create bases in Latvia or go to war, Ulmanis ordered Latvian troops to stand down fearing a bloodbath. Latvia was invaded, and soon arrests, executions, torture and deportations to Siberia befell its citizens. Germany invaded a year later. For the next three years, Latvia was under Nazi occupation, a time during which Latvian Jewry was all but destroyed and men and boys were conscripted into the German army. By the end of the summer of 1944, much of Latvia had been retaken by the Soviets, leading to a mass exodus of refugees to the West. Latvia was illegally annexed by the USSR and remained a captive nation for nearly half a century.

Over the next five decades, collectivisation was enforced and tens of thousands of Latvians were herded like animals into rail boxcars and shipped to Siberia to die. Soviet citizens from around the union were encouraged to move to Latvia in a deliberate attempt to make Latvians a minority in their own nation. Russian

THE FATE OF THE JEWISH GHETTOES

Before World War II there were around 45,000 Jews in Riga, just over ten percent of the population. By 1945 about 150 remained. Several thousand Jews were immediately shot by the Einsatzgruppen (mobile killing units), aided by Latvian auxiliaries, after German troops entered the city in July 1941. The rest were driven into a ghetto behind the station around Lāčplēša and Ludzas streets, which was sealed in October that year. Some 20,000 Jews from Germany, Austria, Bohemia and Moravia were also brought to Riga and sealed in a separate ghetto. Later that year, on just two days, around 25,000 ghetto Jews were murdered in the Rumbula forest 8km (5 miles) southeast of the city. After the war many Jews returned to Latvia and by the time of independence in 1989 there were around 23,000 registered in Riga, though the number has since fallen due to emigration.

became the dominant language of bureaucracy and any displays of patriotism were punished severely. Russian-speakers became the majority in Riga, and unchecked industrial growth polluted the nation's soil and waterways.

The new policies of *glasnost* and *perestroika* introduced by the Soviet President Mikhail Gorbachev gained popularity in the 1980s and inspired Latvians to begin protesting against the regime. Dates of mass deportations to Siberia were commemorated, and activists founded the Latvian Popular Front, which in 1989 called for full independence. That same year, some two million Estonians, Latvians and Lithuanians formed a human chain that stretched from Vilnius to Tallinn to protest the 50th anniversary of the Molotov–Ribbentrop Pact.

In 1991, seizing an opportunity to strike while the world's attention was distracted by the first Gulf War, Soviet troops moved in. In Riga, people erected barricades to protect the parliament, and a Soviet assault on the Interior Ministry resulted in the deaths of five people. In a referendum held in March, Latvians voted overwhelmingly in favour of independence. By 21 August, a coup in Moscow against President Gorbachev had collapsed and the Latvian parliament voted to immediately restore independence, which was recognised by the USSR two weeks later. Latvia was free.

AFTER INDEPENDENCE

The unity experienced during the days of the barricades soon faded and parliament became rife with partisanship, double-dealing and political scandals. Privatisation occurred rapidly, but corruption often benefited individuals and special interests, not the nation as a whole. Latvia's multi-party system led to the creation of unstable coalitions and the parliament presided over the collapse of eleven governments in thirteen years. Fortunately, most parties could agree on two important goals – NATO and the European Union. Latvia became a member of both in 2004.

The 130th Latvian Rifle Corps

The 2008 world financial crisis hit Latvia hard, causing massive unemployment (over twenty percent), a €7.5bn loan from the IMF, followed by drastic austerity measures and the subsequent collapse of the government. The opposition New Age Party took the reins, making tough decisions to save what was left of the economy. Government employee salaries were slashed by nearly half as unemployment soared to over twenty percent. Although the economy rebounded in 2012, mainly due to a strong export market, and in 2014 Latvia adopted the euro, some problems remain, namely high unemployment and a demographic crisis sparked by economic emigration, reducing the country's population to 1.9 million – a loss of over 600,000 citizens since 1989. Geopolitical tensions with Russia over the conflict in Ukraine pose yet another challenge to Latvians fearing that their hard-won independence may be under threat. In 2015, Latvia, together with Lithuania and Estonia, asked for a permanent presence of NATO troops on its soil. Legislation in 2023 brought back military service to bolster the country's armed forces. Edgars Rinkevičs, who as foreign minister had been a strident advocate of increased European security, was

Girls in traditional dress

elected Latvian president in 2023, becoming the EU's first openly gay head of state.

CHRONOLOGY

2500 BC The ancestors of modern Latvians arrive on the Baltic Sea.
1100s German traders appear by the River Daugava.
1201 Bishop Albert founds the city of Riga.
1202 The Livonian Order is created with the pope's blessing in Riga.
1282 Riga joins the Hanseatic League.
1522 The Reformation arrives in Riga, bringing with it social unrest.
1561 The Livonian Order ceases to exist.
1621 Sweden is victorious in Polish-Swedish war. Golden age begins.
1710 Riga surrenders to Peter the Great of Russia.
1819 Serfdom is abolished.
1905 The first Russian Revolution fails and hundreds are executed.
1918 Independence proclaimed by Latvian intelligentsia.
1919 Russian Red forces take Riga and fledgling government flees.
1921 Latvian independence is recognised by the USSR.
1940 The Soviet Union invades Latvia.
1941 The Nazis drive out the Soviets.
1944 The Red Army once again occupies most of Latvia, and at the end of the war Latvia is left on the wrong side of the Iron Curtain.
1989 Latvian Popular Front calls for full independence.
1991 Latvia declares its independence.
1994 The last Soviet troops withdraw.
2004 Latvia joins Nato and the EU.
2008 A €7.5bn package is approved by the IMF and EU. Austerity measures provoke social unrest and the fall of the government.
2014 The euro is adopted, pushing prices up.
2017 NATO Enhanced Forward Presence deployed in Latvia.
2022 Russia's full invasion of Ukraine places the Baltic States at the centre of East-West tension.
2023 Evika Siliņa replaces Arturs Krišjānis Kariņš as prime minister.

Riga's Old Town and
the Dome Cathedral

Places

By Baltic standards Riga is a huge city, but in truth many of its most interesting sights are easily accessible on foot or by a short tram ride. A stroll through the meandering cobblestone streets of Old Riga, a ride to the top of St Peter's spire for fantastic views of terracotta roofs, and a tour of the city centre's incredible Art Nouveau buildings are all highlights of a trip to the Latvian capital. For the sake of expediency, this guide divides the old town into two sections, which are followed by descriptions of the surrounding ring of boulevards and parks. The most noteworthy regions of the city centre or 'new city' have also been listed, as are suburban places of interest. Intrepid travellers can also take excursions to crusader castle ruins and restored palaces in the countryside.

OLD RIGA: SOUTHERN HALF

HIGHLIGHTS

In the eight hundred years since its founding, Riga has experienced dramatic changes at the hands of both foreign armies and local town planners but, for the most part, its winding streets haven't changed their course or, for that matter, their names. Most of the old town's bustling streets and alleyways still bear the names that indicated the trades of their early inhabitants, such as Painters', Merchants' and Blacksmiths' streets.

This tour starts south of Lime Street (Kaļķu iela), the dividing line of Old Riga, where the city began its existence as a small fishing village populated by Liv tribesmen, around what is now **Albert Square** (Alberta laukums).

It certainly isn't one of the prettiest squares the city has to offer but it does provide a unique glimpse of Riga's past, present and future. From here you can view restored seventeenth-century warehouses, Cold War-era Soviet architecture, the crumbling husks of derelict apartment buildings and, in the distance, the glass-and-steel facade of a cinema complex.

Albert Square

ALKSNĀJA, PEITAVAS AND MĀRSTAĻU STREETS

Walk past graffitied warehouses dating from the sixteenth to eighteenth centuries on Alksnāja iela until you reach the **Latvian Sports Museum** (www.sportamuzejs.lv; guided tours only), which celebrates the nation's best athletes. Along the way, note the bas-reliefs of plants and animals above the huge wooden warehouse doors, which informed the mostly illiterate populace of the items stored within: clusters of grapes denoted wines and a camel symbolised spices from the East. Similar signs can be seen throughout Old Riga. Ahead on the left is the **Reformation Church** (Reformātu baznīca), which was built from 1727 to 1733. One of the few Baroque-style houses of worship in the city, for a time it also had the distinction of having the only Calvinist congregation in Latvia. The Soviets used it as a recording studio and student disco, but after independence the ground floor was turned into a concert hall and the cellar became a string of nightclubs.

Across the street is the **Latvian Museum of Photography** (Latvijas fotogrāfijas muzejs; www.fotomuzejs.lv; currently closed for renovations), which has a collection of late nineteenth-century rural landscapes, twentieth-century portraits and some striking images from World War I. The highlight of the museum, a Minox spy camera produced in Latvia just before the war and later manufactured by famous German firm Leica, is currently on show at the Latvian Academy of Arts at Kronvalda 8 (see page 69).

One block over on Peitavas iela is Riga's only surviving **synagogue** (Sinagoga; www.jews.lv; free), built in 1904. It was spared the fate of other Jewish houses of worship due to its close proximity to houses in Old Riga. Fearing an uncontrollable blaze if they torched it, the Nazis used it instead as a warehouse.

Colourful Mārstaļu Street

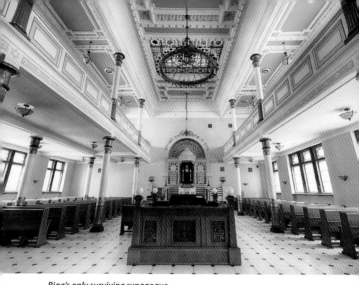

Riga's only surviving synagogue

Further up Mārstaļu, just before the river, you'll see one of the last remaining fragments of the old town's original **city walls** to the left and the **Dannenstern House** on the right. Built in 1696 by a wealthy Dutch merchant, it was the largest residence at the time in Riga. Its owner oversaw a fleet of 150 ships and was later given a noble title by the king of Sweden. Due to a lack of space in the medieval city, most homes also served as warehouses, which is clear to anyone who looks at this massive, multi-storeyed structure. Ahead is the river promenade, which leads to the **1905 Revolution monument** to the left. Nearly two thousand people across Latvia were killed in the aftermath of the failed uprising.

On the opposite end of Mārstaļu is one of the best examples of both Dutch Classical and Baroque architecture in Riga – the **Reutern House** (Reiterna nams), completed in 1685. Look out for the frieze just beneath the roof depicting a lion pouncing on a bear – the owner's cheeky way of celebrating the victory of Sweden over Russia. Today, it often hosts exhibitions.

ST JOHN'S AND BEYOND

Just past the aptly named Sinners' Street (Grēcinieku iela), home to some of the city's hottest nightclubs and bars, you'll see the bright terracotta tiles and green neo-Gothic spire of **St John's Church** (Jāņa baznīca; free), built in the thirteenth century. Like most Lutheran churches, its interior is for the most part austere, but its elaborate vaulted ceiling is considered to be one of the most beautiful in the Baltic region.

Two medieval monks chose to be immured in the southern wall in the hope of becoming saints and were fed by passersby through two window grates that are still visible from the street. They didn't survive long and were never canonised because they did it for their own glory and not for the glory of God. Their bodies were rediscovered in the nineteenth century after the spire collapsed causing minor damage to the building. Repairs were made and they were left behind the wall.

Just behind the building is the picturesque **John's Courtyard** (Jāņa sēta), home to a cluster of bars, clubs and beer gardens. Here you can see another fragment of Riga's

NOTES

Nearly bankrupt and desperate for work, Richard Wagner travelled to Riga in 1837, where he worked as the musical director of the German Theatre, conducted many of Beethoven's symphonies and began writing *Rienzi, the Last of the Tribunes*. After only two seasons, he made a hasty escape from his creditors in 1839, leaving the city for London and Paris under cover of darkness. The stormy waters of the Baltic Sea later served as his inspiration for the *Flying Dutchman*.

*Bremen Town Musicians
political monument*

old town walls, draped with flowers in summer.

Beyond the courtyard at No. 13 on Wagner Street (Vāgnera iela) is the **Museum of Pharmacy** (Farmācijas muzejs; www.mvm.lv), which displays old bottles, many of which still contain their original ingredients. Of equal significance is the building's rococo doorway, one of the few examples of this style in Riga. Further up the street at No. 4 is the **Wagner Concert Hall** (Vāgnera zāle) where the troubled composer conducted for two years (see page 37).

Opposite the church is a statue of the **Bremen Town Musicians** from the Grimms' fairytale. It was a gift from the city of Bremen, another Hanseatic city and home of Bishop Albert (1165–1229), founder of Riga. Just behind the church on the corner of Jāṇa and Kalēju streets is arguably Old Riga's most beautiful Art Nouveau building. Built in 1903, it's a fine example of Biological Romanticism.

The yellow building next to the church is **Ecke's Convent** (Ekes konventa ēka), which once belonged to a Riga mayor of the same name. Embroiled in an embezzlement scandal in 1596, he decided to curry favour with the townspeople by donating the building to impoverished widows. A hotel and teashop now occupy its floors, but its most interesting asset is a bas-relief of Jesus and the Sinner on its facade.

The next building down the street is also a gate to the **Convent Yard** (Konventa sēta), which is an ensemble of several medieval buildings confined by other structures in a quaint courtyard once used to house the impoverished and disabled citizens of Riga. It is now home to an upmarket hotel, shops, cafés and the **Riga Porcelain Museum**  (Rīgas pocelāna muzejs; http://porcelanamuzejs.riga.lv), whose medieval architecture has been carefully restored and whose main claim to fame is an exhibit of nineteenth-century ceramics; it also has a huge vase bearing the likeness of Stalin. For a small charge, children can try their hand at pottery on the premises.

A few houses down the street is the **Museum of Decorative Arts and Design** (Dekoratīvās mākslas un dizaina muzejs; www.lnmm.lv). Of more interest than the actual exhibits is the first building, which was once the chapel of the Livonian Order's castle and the city's first church, St George's (Jura baznīca). The castle was destroyed by the townspeople, but the chapel was unharmed and, to this day, is considered by many Latvians to be a source of supernatural energy.

St Peter's Church steeple

On the other side of the street is Riga's tallest medieval structure, **St Peter's Church**  (Pēterbaznīca; http://peterbaznica.riga.lv). Although the exact date of its construction is unknown, St Peter's was mentioned in chronicles in 1209. It was later enlarged and by 1491 its soaring steeple was completed.

Unfortunately, the steeple was beset by a series of disasters. It collapsed in 1666 killing townspeople below, and a decade into its reconstruction it burned down. When it was finally rebuilt in 1690 it was the tallest wooden church steeple in Europe, but it was once again engulfed in flames in 1721. Peter the Great, who was visiting Riga at the time, ordered the steeple to be rebuilt, and by 1746 it reached an impressive height of 127m (415ft).

The architect drank a glass of wine at the top and dropped it to the ground, believing that the number of shards it broke into would be the number of centuries it would survive. Sadly, a pile of hay softened the blow, and it only broke in two. Nearly two

The House of Blackheads at night

centuries later in 1941, it was hit by a bomb and collapsed in flames. The current steeple was completed in 1973, and the ritual was repeated – to the delight of all, the glass smashed into thousands of pieces. You can take the lift (charge) up to the observation deck for excellent views and visit the church and the crypt.

Further up the road is a lovely building topped with Dionysus holding a cluster of grapes. It was here that the Jewish-American photographer Philippe Halsman (1906–79), friend of Albert Einstein and Salvador Dalí, lived until 1929. It also has the distinction of being the first of many Art Nouveau buildings built in Riga.

St Peter's Church

TOWN HALL SQUARE

To the left you'll see the Baroque-style tower of the reconstructed **Town Hall** (Rātsnams), completed in 2004. The original building, dating from 1334, was demolished in 1750 to make room for a larger structure. Like most of the ancient square, which served as both marketplace and punishment venue, it was levelled during World War II.

This recreation of the original building – with additional third floor and modern wing – is once again the seat of city government. A subterranean passageway is home to shops and a 3500-year-old section of an oak tree found under the building's foundations.

Latvian riflemen monument

In the centre of the square is a statue of **St Roland** (Rolands) clad in a suit of armour, holding a sword in one hand and a shield bearing Riga's coat of arms in the other. Dying a martyr's death at the Battle of Roncesvals in 778, he was Charlemagne's favourite nephew and came to symbolise justice in many cities inhabited by Germans, of which Riga was no exception. The original statue was slightly damaged during the war and is on display in St Peter's Church, safe from the elements.

Behind Roland is the **House of Blackheads** Ⓒ (Melngalvju nams), another building to rise from the ashes of Soviet bombings. The fourteenth-century original once housed a guild of unmarried merchants whose bacchanalian feasts became the stuff of legend. It is rumoured that monarchs and nobility, including Catherine the Great, secretly participated in these events. Most scholars believe that the ancient building derives its name from either the black caps worn by its early members or from its patron saint Mauritius, a Moor.

Behind the building on the corner is the **Mentzendorff House** (Mencendorfa nams; www.mencendorfanams.com), dating from 1695. It illustrates the lifestyle of seventeenth- and eighteenth-century Riga merchants. During restoration, builders discovered wonderful frescoes on the walls and ceilings under layers of Soviet paint. The interior was completed with historical artefacts from the Museum of the History of Riga and Navigation.

Back on the square is the unmistakable Soviet black box constructed in 1970 as a museum dedicated to the Latvian Red Riflemen who fought during the Russian Civil War. Today, its austere architecture provides an appropriate venue for the chilling **Museum of the Occupation of Latvia** ⓓ (Latvijas okupācijas muzejs; http://okupacijasmuzejs.lv; charge). Inside you'll find documents, photographs and exhibits that chronicle Latvia's occupation by the Soviet Union and Nazi Germany. A gulag barracks has also been reconstructed to illustrate the terrible living conditions many Latvians faced after being deported to Siberia in cattle cars.

On the other side of the museum is a red granite monument now dedicated to all the **Latvian riflemen** who fought during World War I. Desperate for more troops, the tsar allowed the creation of a Latvian army to fight against the Germans, but when the revolution broke out some joined the Reds. An elite few of the Latvian Red Riflemen became the private bodyguard of Lenin. Soldiers from both sides joined Latvia's cause after independence was declared in 1918.

Beside the monument you can sign up for organised walking and bus tours of the city.

Latvia's steeple-pierced skyline

OLD RIGA: NORTHERN HALF

HIGHLIGHTS

» Dome Square (Doma laukums), see page 46
» Art Museum Riga Bourse, see page 49
» Around Dome Square, see page 50
» Riga Castle, see page 52
» Livs' Square, see page 57

Just before the Town Hall Square is Trash Street (Krāmu iela), which, contrary to its misguided name, affords passersby one of the most picturesque views of Dome Cathedral. Heading towards the church on the right side is Riga's narrowest street, **Rozena iela**, which is made more picturesque by a medieval-style restaurant. On the right is the **Museum of Barricades of 1991** (1991. gada barikāžu muzejs; http://barikades.lv; free), which tells the story of how Latvians from across the country flocked to the city to protect it against elite Soviet OMON forces in January and August 1991. Giant concrete slabs were erected around Old Riga and lorry drivers and even farmers on tractors deposited their vehicles at strategic locations to deny tanks entry. Around the corner on Jauniela is another excellent example of Art Nouveau, built in 1903 and famous for its huge face above the entrance. Across the street in a courtyard once used as a beer garden you can see **tombstones** that paved the floor of the cathedral. In the left corner is a small bas-relief of the crucifixion painted silver, which is also believed to have once been

> ## NOTES
>
> When Russian troops captured Riga in 1710, it was a huge feather in Peter the Great's cap. The tsar is said to have visited the city often and was given a gift of a palace by the local magistrate, which is still visible, albeit in modified form, at No. 9 Palasta in Old Riga.

Dome Square

located indoors. Below you can see the ground level of Riga before floods, fires and eight hundred years of habitation took their toll.

Ahead is a former palace built in the late 1600s (and reconstructed several times), which has played host to eighteenth- and nineteenth-century royalty, including Peter the Great and Catherine the Great. Beyond the palace is a tiny shed which is probably the only medieval carriage house in Riga still in existence.

Just before **Herder Square** (Herdera laukums), named after the influential German philosopher Johann Gotfried Herder (1744–1803) who once taught at the Dome School, is one of the country's best and oldest museums, the **Museum of the History of Riga and Navigation** (Rīgas vēstures un kuģniecības muzejs; www. rigamuz.lv; charge). The first public museum in the Balkans when it opened in 1773, it was based on the collection of Nikolaus von

---

BISHOP ALBERT

Albert von Buxhoevden (1165–1229) is credited with the founding of Riga in 1201 when he ordered the construction of a fortification to protect himself and his crusaders from local pagan tribes. Born into a prominent family – the Buxhoevdens of northern Germany – he was a member of the clergy in Bremen before being named bishop of Livonia.

Eager to avoid the fate of his predecessor, who was torn to pieces in a battle with a Liv tribe, he garnered the support of Pope Innocent III and King Philip of Swabia. He also obtained a papal bull to save the souls of the heathens living in the northern Baltic. With 23 ships and an army of 1500 men, he arrived in what would become Riga.

Previous attempts to subdue the local Latvian tribes had failed. In 1202, Bishop Albert founded the Livonian Order, a permanent military monastic order that was based on the Templars. The order did battle across Latvia and parts of Estonia, building castles as they went.

By his death in 1229 Albert had founded a city and an order of knights, built fortresses and the Dome Cathedral, and attained the titles of Holy Roman Prince and Bishop of Livonia. A statue of the illustrious clergyman adorns one of the walls of the Dome Cloister.

Himsel, a medical practitioner who had died nine years earlier at the age of 35, and moved into the current building in 1891. Inside is an eclectic collection of all things Rigan (though, ironically, not much to do with the sea), including Bronze Age artefacts, suits of armour, religious items, medieval documents, memorabilia from the 1920s and 1930s, and plenty of other curiosities.

DOME SQUARE (DOMA LAUKUMS)

Seven streets converge at this beautiful square that is now the heart and soul of Old Riga. Yet, oddly, it didn't even exist only a century ago. Ancient houses once covered the square, some of which were demolished by the city to grant greater access to the cathedral, and the rest fell victim to bombing raids during World War II. Today, if you look closely at the patterns of the cobblestones you can discern the outlines of the buildings that once stood in the shadow of the largest house of worship in the Baltics. In the centre of the square is a bronze disc commemorating the city's inclusion on UNESCO's list of World Heritage Sites. It is also at this point that you can see three church spires.

Construction of **Dome Cathedral** Ⓔ (Rīgas Doms or Doma baznīca; www.doms.lv) began at the behest of Riga's founder, Bishop Albert (see page 46), in 1211, but like all of the city's churches it was enlarged and embellished over the years. In fact, steps lead down to the north door because the city's constant

The cathedral's original weathervane

rebuilding has meant the ground level has actually risen over the years. Even the golden numerals on the east side of the building, indicating the year 1721, only give evidence of the completion of repairs to the church, which suffered during Peter the Great's siege of the city in 1709. It was also damaged by a devastating flood that same year and a small plaque on the far right side of the church before the altar marks the level that the water reached. Its many treasures were looted during the Reformation riots of the 1520s and its elaborately carved pews (apart from the Blackheads' pew depicting Moors) 'disappeared' during its reconstruction as a concert hall during the Soviet era. Thankfully, many of the original stained-glass windows donated by the guilds and wealthy patrons have survived.

Art Museum Riga Bourse

One of the cathedral's most valuable assets is its enormous **organ** embellished with ornate wood carvings. The original instrument was installed in the late sixteenth century and served its parishioners well for nearly three hundred years until the congregation decided to commission a better one. Even the tsar donated money to the cause and by 1884 the continent's best-known firm, Walcker's of Ludwigsburg, completed the task of building the world's largest organ. The dedication was such a momentous event that Franz Liszt composed music for the occasion. The wood carvings from the 1590s were not replaced and can still be viewed today. Organ concerts are held here frequently.

Behind the cathedral is a courtyard and the **Dome Cloister** (Doma krusteja; www.rigamuz.lv), encircled by a 118-metre (387ft) vaulted gallery, one of the most outstanding examples of north European medieval construction work. Apart from excellent examples of Romanesque architecture, you can also view various outdoors exhibits, including an old canon, the cathedral's original copper rooster weathervane, tombstones dating back to the thirteenth century and even a stained-glass depiction of Lenin.

Dome Cathedral isn't the only architectural gem on the square. Perhaps the most striking building is the Venetian Renaissance-style **Stock Exchange** (Rīgas birža) building, completed in 1855 and painted in various shades of brown and green, now housing the excellent **Art Museum Riga Bourse** (Mākslas muzejs Rīgas Birža; http://lnmm.lv; charge). The opulent gallery exhibits include a superb collection of seventeenth-century North European

Riga Castle

school paintings as well as eighteenth-century Meissen porcelain. There is also a museum shop and café.

Opposite the museum is the **Radio House** (Radio māja), built in 1913, with the coat of arms of Riga above the balcony where heads of state, including former and current presidents of Latvia, have given speeches to the masses below. It now houses offices and studios for Latvian Radio. At the east end of the square are some more examples of fantastic Art Nouveau architecture, as well as a wide variety of shops and cafés.

AROUND DOME SQUARE

Every street around the square reveals yet another medieval or Art Nouveau treasure. Head for the sky-blue church at the end of Pils and you'll be rewarded with vibrant cafés and more beautiful buildings. On the left is the odd-looking Danish embassy and the tiny Anglican church, **St Saviour's** (Anglikāņu baznīca). In 1857, wealthy British businessmen imported soil and bricks from England to build this small church, which still delivers services to its expatriate congregation in English.

Proceed to **Castle Square** (Pils laukums) where you'll see the bright blue **Church of Our Lady of Sorrow** (Sāpju Dievmātes katoļu baznīca). In the eighteenth century, the only Catholic church in Old Riga was a tiny wooden chapel that occupied this space. Austria's Kaiser Joseph II was horrified to see such a poor representation of his faith and donated a large sum of money to build the church you see now. Sadly, the Kaiser died in ignominy and subsequent royalty who donated to the church all died violent deaths, including Tsar Alexander II who was blown up by anarchists. The church was completed in 1785.

If you take the small street, Poļu gāte, behind the church to the river you'll see the **Big Christopher** statue. Legend has it that after carrying a small boy across the river, who was in fact the Christ child, St Christopher returned to his cave on the embankment and discovered a pile of gold, which he used to build the city. A wooden statue first appeared by the river in the early sixteenth century and served as Riga's protector against the extremes of nature, especially floods. Riga's citizens would also leave offerings to him to ensure a safe journey. The current statue, encased in glass, is a replica of the original now located in the Museum of the History of Riga and Navigation.

WHERE TO SHOOT THE BEST PICTURES

The medieval Riga Castle – one of the largest in Latvia and now home to the President of Latvia – can be appreciated (and photographed) from afar. The entire castle is best captured from the bank of the River Daugava. Another architectural showstopper is the gold-domed Nativity of Christ Cathedral, a neo-Byzantine Russian Orthodox cathedral (the largest of its kind in the Baltic provinces) in the heart of the city. While long-term restorations work on its interiors, snap a photo of its imposing facade from the skyline bar of the *Radisson Hotel*. And, of course, you can't capture Riga in all its glory without snapping its Art Nouveau beauties. Head to Albert Street to home in on rich and colourful Art Nouveau ornamentation by renowned Russian architect Mikhail Eisenstein or wander to 10a Elizabetes Street to photograph work by the most prolific architect of the period, Konstantīns Pēkšēns.

The centrepiece of the square is, of course, the ancient Crusader Castle of the Livonian Order or **Riga Castle** (Rīgas pils). After the townspeople destroyed their first castle in 1297, the Order gained the upper hand and forced the citizens of Riga to build them a new fortress at this location in 1330. It was razed again in 1484, but the relentless Order returned to power and yet again forced the humiliated locals to rebuild it in 1491. Over the years it was expanded and served as the seat of the governors of each invading power, until independence after World War I when Latvian presidents used the building as their offices – a tradition that continues today. In 2011, a fire destroyed parts of the structure, including the Red Hall. Fortunately, the museum art collections stashed inside weren't damaged.

The iconic Three Brothers

If you take Jēkaba iela from Dome Square, make a left on Mazā pils to see an ensemble of three narrow medieval buildings, each erected in a different century, collectively known as the **Three Brothers** ❻ (Trīs brāļi). No. 17 is the oldest residential building in the city, dating back to the fifteenth century. The bench outside gives an indication of the house's age; successive generations of homeowners could not afford to set aside space indoors in which to relax. No. 17's windows are tiny to avoid the

Powder Tower

'light tax' of the time that forced residents to pay more for windows that cast a glow on the street. No. 19 was built in 1646 and now houses the small but interesting **Latvian Architecture Museum** (Latvijas arhitektūras muzejs; www.archmuseum.lv; free). No. 21 is the most recent addition to the trio.

To the right on Klostera is the building that formerly housed the **Riga Lyceum**, founded by King Charles XI of Sweden in 1675. Above the doorway you'll notice the original crown of the king and a second crown of Peter the Great above it. The tsar couldn't resist the temptation to flaunt his victory over his Scandinavian foe.

Beyond the lyceum is the red-brick **St Jacob's Cathedral** (Jēkaba baznīca; free), first mentioned in historical documents in 1225, the date engraved above its entrance portal. In 1522 it became the first church in Latvia to hold a Lutheran service, but sixty years later,

The Swedish Gate

when the Polish King Stephen Bathory took the city for a brief spell, it was handed to the Catholics. Its 73-metre (240ft) thin green spire, topped by a gold cockerel, is one of the three cloud-raking steeples that shape the city's skyline. Note the bell hanging on the outside of the cathedral; like most of the city's treasures made of precious metals, the bell was carted off to Russia and melted down during World War I, but was replaced by a new one in 2001.

Outside the church on Jēkaba stands one of the concrete slabs used to protect the parliament from Soviet tanks in 1991. The **Latvian Parliament** (Latvijas Republikas Saeima) building can be seen to the north of the cathedral. Constructed in 1867 as a meeting hall for the German landed gentry who could trace their line-ages back to crusading knights, it is now used by the descendants of the very people it tried to oppress. The building is closed to the public, but is impressive to look at from the outside. Particularly imposing are the iron chains surrounding the building which hang from the mouths of miniature lions' heads. Indeed, all of its features are massive, including the giant doorknockers and lampposts.

Behind the parliament is the **Arsenāls Exhibition Hall** of the Latvian National Museum of Art (Izstāžu zāle Arsenāls; www.lnmm. lv), housed in an impressive nineteenth-century customs warehouse, Riga's finest example of Russian Classicism. Most of the exhibits, including paintings by Latvian expatriates, are from the second half of the twentieth century to the present.

If you head down Smilšu, one of the city's oldest streets, you'll see some excellent examples of early twentieth-century architecture, most notably at Nos 2 and 8. The former was built in 1902 and exemplifies the trend of Biological Romanticism in Art Nouveau. With a huge peacock, trees and human forms that have roots in place of legs, the building seems almost alive. No. 8, erected in the same year, is covered with faces, gargoyles and cherubs, and has two naked women on either side of the main balcony. Make sure to take a peek at the elaborate floral designs inside the foyer.

At the end of the street is the **Powder Tower** (Pulvertornis), which may have stored gunpowder during medieval times. Dating back as far as the fourteenth century, it was almost completely destroyed by invading Swedish troops in 1621. It was rebuilt thirty years later with 2.5m (8ft)-thick walls to avoid a repeat of this calamity. Its new construction proved successful and cheeky local masons showed off their achievement

The Small Guild

by embedding cannonballs that failed to penetrate the structure in its exterior. By the end of the nineteenth century, the tower had been long abandoned until a German student fraternity convinced the town council to rent them the building for a token one rouble per year. The canny pupils made a killing by selling the pigeon droppings that had piled up over decades of disuse as fertiliser. Today, the tower is a part of the **Latvian Museum of War** (Latvijas kara muzejs; charge), which chronicles the evolution of the Latvian army during the twentieth century.

To the left on Aldaru, beyond the gravity-defying warehouse that leans over the street, is the 1698-built **Swedish Gate** ◐ (Zviedru vārti), the only gate remaining in the city walls, and through it the condemned were led to their fate. Note the cannon embedded in the corners. Passing in front of the gate is Noise

Street (Trokšņu iela), one of the city's narrowest and most picturesque streets.

To the right is the largest fragment of the once massive **old city fortress walls**. The **Ramer Guard Tower** was reconstructed during the Soviet era, so the smooth bricks betray the tower's youth, but the sight is still impressive. **Jacob's Barracks** (Jēkaba kazarmas), on the other side of the street, were built to house Swedish soldiers in the eighteenth century and continued to serve that function until Latvia regained its independence in 1991. Today they represent one of the most expensive pieces of real estate in the old town and are occupied by some of the city's trendiest shops and cafés, not to mention diplomats who live in its exclusive apartments.

LIVS' SQUARE

Although it is now one of the city's most beautiful open spaces, teeming with people, shops, cafés, beer gardens and buskers, **Livs' Square** (Līvu laukums) didn't exist prior to World War II, when the ancient buildings of the area were bombed beyond recognition. This is the best place for people watching in summer and also a great destination for soaking up the atmosphere of Old Riga.

On the western side of the square are the guildhalls, the seats of ultimate power in the city until Russian economic

Cat House

policies made them completely impotent in 1877. They did, however, continue to exist as a kind of German social club until Hitler ordered all of his Volk to return to the fatherland in the late 1930s.

The **Small Guild** (Mazā Ģilde) was built during the fourteenth century as a centre for the city's highly skilled artisans, but the present neo-Gothic structure, with its fairytale tower, was not erected until 1866. Its interior is decorated with unique tapestries and stained glass, as well as the coats of arms of several Hanseatic cities. It served various functions during Soviet times, but is now once again home to the city's Craftsmen's Guild and is also used for conferences, concerts and other special events.

The **Great Guild** (Lielā Ģilde) was home to Riga's wealthy power-brokers, who laid down the law for all economic activities in the city.

Kronvalda Park

Only merchants who didn't work for wages could be admitted and the ban on the acceptance of non-German members was lifted only in the second half of the nineteenth century when the old fourteenth-century hall was replaced by the current fortress-like neo-Gothic structure. Thankfully, the ancient Münster hall, which was the venue of countless medieval events, was untouched during the upgrade. It is now used as a concert hall and is home to the Latvian Philharmonic Orchestra.

The so-called **Cat House** (Kaķu nams), whose

image appears on countless postcards and t-shirts, is located across the street. Its striking yellow facade is reason enough to stop and look, but it's the slender black felines perched at the top of the building's towers that are the source of its fame and infamy. The story goes that the wealthy merchant who owned the building was involved in a squabble with the Great Guild and, although he fulfilled all the necessary requirements, was denied membership in the prestigious organisation. In protest, he had the cats on the towers

National Theatre

moved so that their backsides faced the guild. The guildsmen, who were the most influential citizens of the city, were outraged at the insult, but were, perhaps for the first time in their lives, completely powerless and could do nothing to convince their adversary to tame his unruly pets. Today the cats face the philharmonic hall.

CITY CENTRE

HIGHLIGHTS

Riga's massive fortress walls and earthen ramparts have faithfully protected the city for half a millennium, but by the nineteenth century they had outlived their usefulness. Modern warfare had rendered them obsolete, and Riga was quickly becoming one of the largest and wealthiest cities in the Russian Empire. Riga's most affluent citizens were tired of living in cramped conditions in the old town, where the filth and grime of urban living was taking its toll on the population. A change was needed. The desolate land that lay directly beyond the walls would be turned into artfully landscaped parks, the archaic fortifications torn down, the ramparts destroyed and the ban on the construction of stone buildings outside Old Riga lifted. The stage was set for the largest and most far-reaching construction boom in the city's history and the result is the magnificent semicircle of parks and boulevards that surrounds the medieval core of Riga, and the priceless Art Nouveau masterpieces of the city centre.

KRONVALDA PARK

Named after Atis Kronvalds (1837–75), the Latvian linguist and teacher who later came to symbolise the National Awakening in the second half of the nineteenth century, this extensive park is divided in two by the city canal and is a favourite spot for reading a book on its many benches, feeding ducks at the water's edge, in-line skating on its smoothly paved walkways or simply basking in the sun. For some seventy years this prime piece of real estate between Elizabetes, Valdemāra, Kronvalda and Kalpaka boulevards was the exclusive domain of a German shooting club which created an entertainment complex that charged admission at the main entrance. The city of Riga finally bought the park in 1931 for the benefit of all its citizens and visitors.

On the northern side of the canal is Riga's **World Trade Centre**, formerly the home of the Central Committee of the Communist Party of Latvia, which currently houses embassies and international firms. Not far from the building you'll notice a concrete slab on display. It is a fragment of the **Berlin Wall**, which was donated to the city by the museum at Checkpoint Charlie. The park also displays several other different monuments, including a small pagoda (a gift from the Chinese Embassy), and the only remaining pavilion from Riga's 700th anniversary celebrations in 1901.

At the southernmost tip of the park on Valdemāra is the **National Theatre** (Nacionālais teātris) where Latvian independence was declared in November 1918 (see page 27). The building, which

Statue of Mother Latvia at the Freedom Monument

was designed by Augusts Reinbergs and dates back to 1902, now has a modern addition in the rear, as well as a restored Art Nouveau and Classicist interior.

On the other side of Kronvalda is the area of Riga where the medieval **Citadel** (Citadele) once stood. The massive fortifications thwarted the invasions of one Russian tsar and two Polish kings, but by the early eighteenth century its days were numbered. During the siege of 1709, which lasted several months, the Swedish garrison confidently held its ground until the warehouse storing all its gunpowder was hit by artillery. The blast completely destroyed the fortress and at least a thousand people died in an instant. Under the Russians, the Citadel was rebuilt, but only a few of the original buildings exist today.

Sts Peter and Paul Church (Pētera un Pāvila baznīca) was constructed in 1785 as an Orthodox house of worship for Russian soldiers, but was later turned into a concert hall, which is currently named Ave Sol. In the courtyard stands the bust of Anna Kern. The wife of a local general who lived nearby, she was the inspiration for much of Alexander Pushkin's love poetry.

Sandwiched between the foreign representations on Kalpaka, or 'embassy row', on the opposite side of the park is the **Paul Stradiņš Museum of the History of Medicine** (Paula Stradiņa medicīnas vēstures muzejs; www.mvm.lv). The museum bears the name of Latvia's most illustrious physician and professor, Paul Stradiņš (1896–1958), and traces the history of medical practice from medieval to modern times. Among the intriguing exhibits is medical equipment that looks as if it did more harm than good and old signs warning of smallpox epidemics.

FREEDOM MONUMENT AND RIGA CANAL

A large statue of Peter the Great astride a horse once occupied the space where Latvia's most sacred monument now stands. When the tsar's statue went missing during World War I, the Latvians were in no rush to get it back. After donations were collected from all corners of the country, the **Freedom Monument ❶** (Brīvības piemineklis), referred to endearingly by locals as Milda, was unveiled in 1935 to much fanfare. Designed by Latvian sculptor Kārlis Zāle, the tall white obelisk is topped by the statue of Mother Latvia holding three golden stars representing the historic regions of the country: Kurzeme, Vidzeme and Latgale. A simple inscription reads 'For fatherland and freedom'. The rest is richly ornamented with sculptures and reliefs depicting both historic events and characters from Latvian mythology, from the epic hero Lāčplēsis (the Bear Slayer) in battle and the Song Festival march to the 1905 Revolution and the freedom fighters of 1919. Since its inauguration, the monument has gained the status of a national shrine, and flowers are placed at its foot each day, an act that was punishable by deportation to Siberia in Soviet times.

Before you reach the monument on Aspazijas you'll see dozens of people milling about in front of the **Laima Clock** (Laimas pulkstenis). This has been Riga's most popular meeting place since the clock bearing the name of the famous chocolate factory was erected in 1924.

To the left of the monument is **Bastion Hill** (Bastejkalns), a man-made mound created in the nineteenth century on a previously flat parcel of land with the earth of the archaic ramparts. Several winding paths lead to the top of the hill, from which there would be a great view were it not for the dozens of trees that surround it. Ornamental fragments of historic houses destroyed during World War II have been added to the park in several places. Scattered before and beyond the pedestrian bridge are five granite memorial stones bearing the names of the film photographers and police officers gunned down by Soviet troops in January 1991.

Bastion Hill sculpture

On the right side of the Freedom Monument is the **National Opera House** ❶ (Latvijas Nacionālā opera; www.opera.lv) and gardens, the pride and joy of Riga. Once known as the German Theatre, it was the first building in Riga to be electrified, after a gas leak nearly destroyed it. The tall

LATVIAN FOLK SONGS

Latvians sing while they work, while they play, at sombre occasions and at celebrations. Apart from their language and love of nature, Latvians are most proud of their folk songs, called *dainas*, which have been passed down from one generation to the next. The songs embody the wisdom of their ancestors and expound on subjects as diverse as farming, religion, funeral rites and sex.

Among the earliest students of folk songs in Latvia was the German philosopher Johann Gotfried Herder (1744–1803), whose studies inspired his belief that a feeling of belonging to one's nation is one of the most basic of human needs. Eventually nineteenth-century Latvian intellectuals recognised the value of the *dainas* and began transcribing them, most notably Krišjānis Barons (1835–1923). He travelled around the countryside, often on foot, collecting these treasures and painstakingly recording them for posterity. He began publishing *dainas* in 1895 and by 1915 the collection had reached 217,996 songs. His work was continued long after his death and today the number of texts has swollen to nearly 1.2 million songs with nearly 30,000 melodies, one of the largest bodies of oral folklore in the world.

There are around 150 folk-song choirs in Latvia, and former president Vaira Vīķe-Freiberga is the author of two books on the subject, *Saules dainas* and *Linguistics and Poetics of Latvian Folk Songs*.

smokestack next to the canal was a part of the power station that provided the energy to light the inside of the theatre and the surrounding neighbourhood – no mean feat in 1887. The nymph fountain and gardens were created the following year to celebrate the building's grand re-opening. Now home to the Riga opera and ballet companies, its opulent interior and stage, once graced by native sons Mikhail Baryshnikov and Boris Gudunov, are among Europe's greatest treasures.

On the opposite side of the canal is the **University of Latvia** (Latvijas Universitāte; www.lu.lv), which has been an institution of higher learning since 1869. The footbridge that crosses the canal was a posthumous gift from one of its professors, who in his will stipulated its construction so that students would have no excuse to be late for class. The nearby **Bergs Bazaar** (www.bergabazars. lv) is a stylish village-like enclave built between 1887 and 1900, and one of Riga's premier shopping and dining destinations. Local boutiques offer both local and international items: handmade chocolates, stylish clothing, current and historical maps, beautiful soaps, Latvian linens, delectable pastries, French wine, and much more. On Saturdays there is an excellent farmers' market.

WÖHRMANN PARK

One of the oldest parks in Riga, **Wöhrmann Park** (Vērmanes dārzs) was created on a piece of land donated to the city by Anna

The National Opera House

G. Wöhrmann following its devastation. This was caused by the ill-advised torching of the suburbs in advance of an attack by Napoleon's troops in 1812 that never materialised. The kiosks located at the corners of the park and the main building date back to the nineteenth century when they were used as fruit stands and a mineral-water pavilion, respectively. It is still one of Riga's favourite patches of green and its benches are often crowded with young and old, while the renovated amphitheatre is usually occupied by dozens of Russian pensioners playing chess and chatting.

There are several sights and historic buildings worth seeing around the park. On Merķeļa you can see the facade of the **Latvian Society House** (Latviešu biedrības nams), decorated with an impressive Art Nouveau fresco. Painted by one of Latvia's

Chess in Wöhrmann Park

finest artists, Janis Rozentāls, the fresco depicts ancient Latvian gods. The Latvian Society was instrumental in the creation of the Latvian state and it sponsored schools, seminars, literary works and choirs. In 1873, the Society also sponsored the first Latvian song festival. Further down the street is the **Riga Circus** (Rīgas cirks), the only permanent circus in the Baltics. Built in 1889, it was the first establishment to show silent films in Riga, and today it still fulfils its initial purpose of dazzling young and old with its artistic exhibitions and acrobatic performances. The circus thankfully phased out the use of wild animals in its performances by 2020, following a request from the Ministry of Culture.

On Barona you can visit the **Natural History Museum** (Latvijas dabas muzejs; www.dabasmuzejs.gov.lv; charge), one of the oldest museums in the city. Inside are thousands of items ranging from the curiosities of taxidermy to exotic butterflies and, for the more macabre, pickled body parts. The museum's rarest exhibit is a collection of fossilised fish dating back hundreds of millions of years.

It is also worth pausing while on Barona to see a museum dedicated to the man after whom the street was named. You can view the **Krišjānis Barons Museum** (Krišjāņa Barona memoriālais dzīvoklis; www.baronamuzejs.lv) where the fabled collector of Latvian folk songs lived and worked for the last four years of his life. He died in 1923.

THE ESPLANADE

In the eighteenth century one of Riga's only natural hills covered the area that now comprises the **Esplanade Park** (Esplanāde). However, in 1784, following a devastating bombardment from this elevated position, it was decided to completely level the ancient mound. The sandy expanse was used at first by the military for training and parades, but was later transformed into a luscious park that hosted major events and fairs, including Riga's 700th anniversary celebrations in 1901.

Today the Esplanade is known for three monumental buildings, the most spectacular of which is the **Russian Orthodox Cathedral**  (Pareizticīgo katedrāle), completed in 1884. In an era when all other languages but Russian were officially suppressed, this church was to symbolise the power of the 'true faith' in the Baltics. Its five gilded cupolas and adjoining belfry no doubt made an impression just as they do today. Sadly, when the Soviets converted the building into a planetarium, they destroyed many of the cathedral's frescoes, the work of the day's best artists. The cathedral has returned to its congregation and is still undergoing long-term renovation. Nearby on Brīvības Bulvāris 32, the **National History Museum of Latvia** (Latvijas Nacionālais vēstures muzejs; http://lnvm.lv; charge), which was moved from Rīga castle after the fire there. Exhibits provide an overview of the evolution of the Latvian nation from the Stone Age to the nineteenth century and beyond. Situated across the park on Valdemāra is the massive Baroque-style building that is home to the **Latvian National Museum of Art** (Latvijas Nacionālais mākslas muzejs; www.lnmm.lv; charge), built in 1905. Almost as interesting as the permanent exhibits of paintings by eighteenth-century Baltic German artists and the Latvian masters Rozentāls, Annuss, Valters, Padegs and Liberts,

National History Museum of Latvia

are the frescoes in the main hall painted by the nation's most revered artist, Vilhelms Purvītis. Standing outside the museum is a **statue of Janīs Rozentāls** (1866–1916), whose painting *Leaving the Cemetery* is displayed inside and should not be missed.

Not far from the National Art Museum is the ivy-clad, brick neo-Gothic **Latvian Academy of Arts** (Latvijas Mākslas akadēmija), also built in 1905.

Just off the park on Skolas is **Jews in Latvia** (Ebreji Latvijā; www.jewishmuseum.lv; donations requested), a museum dedicated to the achievements of the Latvian Jewish community, its destruction during the Nazi occupation during World War II, and its revival after the war and regaining of independence in 1991.

ART NOUVEAU DISTRICT

The entire city centre can be described as an outdoor art gallery, with one-third of the **Art Nouveau district ❶** in this flamboyant style. Elizabetes, Antonijas, Strēlnieku, Vīlandes and especially Albert streets are particularly blessed with this optimistic form of architecture. Two factors sparked this phenomenon. Riga's wealth was at its zenith at the end of the nineteenth century and the years preceding World War I, which happened to coincide with the popularity of this expressive art style. And, though hundreds of German cities also had an abundance of these buildings, many were razed during World War II, yet most of Riga's Art Nouveau gems miraculously survived invasions by both Nazis and Soviets.

10a Elizabetes, by Mikhail Eisenstein

Start your tour at No. 33 Elizabetes, the beige building designed by Mikhail Eisenstein (1867–1921) that looks like an elaborate wedding cake. Across the street at No. 10b is perhaps his most well-known work, easily recognised by the incredibly long human faces on either side of a peacock – the symbol of Art Nouveau. Next door at No. 10a is yet another of the architect's buildings that displays hints of Biological Romanticism and some of the most bizarrely shaped windows in the city. Proceed to **Albert Street Ⓜ** (Alberta iela) where nearly all of the buildings are not only Art Nouveau, but also designed by Eisenstein (the entire right side plus No. 13 opposite). After years of neglect during the Soviet era, many of the buildings have been renovated. At the end of the street is Strēlnieku iela, with another Eisenstein masterpiece at No. 4a, which has his typical bright blue touch. On the corner of Alberta and Strēlnieku is **Riga Art Nouveau Museum** (Rīgas Jūgendstila muzejs, www.jugendstils.riga.lv; charge), in what used to be the house of the Latvian architect Konstantīns Pēkšēns. The ground floor is intended to look like the original apartment, which Pēkšēns designed himself. All seven rooms, including the bathroom and kitchen, contain Art Nouveau fixtures and furniture.

On the top floor is the **Janis Rozentāls and Rūdolfs Blaumanis Museum** (Jaņa Rozentāla un Rūdolfa Blaumaņa muzejs; http://memorialiemuzeji.lv; charge), the former apartment of celebrated painter Rozentāls (1866–1916) and his friend, the famous playwright Blaumanis. Even if these Latvian cultural icons have no meaning for you, it's worth looking inside at the elaborate Art Nouveau staircase and interior. There are several other noteworthy buildings of this style two blocks over on Vīlandes.

LATGALE NEIGHBOURHOOD

HIGHLIGHTS

» Central Market, see page 72
» Spiķeri, see page 73

For centuries, ethnic Russians have inhabited this district of Riga, formerly known as Moscow District (Maskavas forštate). Among the oldest of its communities are the Old Believers, a religious group that fled to the area in the late seventeenth century to escape persecution in Russia. The area beyond the five pavilions of the Central Market was also a vibrant centre of Riga's Jewish life, which was brutally extinguished under the Nazis. Unlike the orderly German-influenced streets and manicured parks of the city centre, the **Latgale neighbourhood** (Latgales priekšpilsēta) always had a wild streak and character all its own. Its nineteenth-century wooden houses and Art Nouveau buildings have yet to benefit from the city's economic boom, but the shopping malls, restaurants and exclusive car dealerships on the previously unde-veloped land adjacent to Krasta Street are a testament to the area's potential value.

CENTRAL MARKET

Beyond the railway station are the giant Zeppelin hangars sheltering the **Central Market**  (Centrāltirgus; www.rct.lv; daily 7am–6pm), built by the Germans in southwestern Latvia in World War I and brought here in the 1920s. Upon completion in 1930, it was one of the largest covered markets in Europe and to this day each of its huge pavilions still sells its originally intended products: fish, dairy, fruit and vegetables, and meat. Pick up freshly prepared sauerkraut, pickled garlic, dried herbs and mushrooms, smoked

The Latgale neighbourhood, formerly Moscow District

fish, fancy cakes and tins of sardines. Although it has become a tourist destination, many of its employees are not used to being photographed, so tread lightly and be cautious of pickpockets. The warehouse quarter known as **Spiķeri** just beyond the Central Market on Maskavas street has become a trendy place full of cafes, bars, clubs and art galleries housed in renovated yellow brick buildings. At Maskavas 14a (entrance from Krasta st.) is the eye-opening **Riga Ghetto and Latvian Holocaust Museum**

Stalinist architecture

(Rīgas Geto muzejs; www.rgm.lv), commemorating the victims of the Holocaust.

Further up Prāgas is the **Academy of Sciences** (Zinātņu akadēmija). Designed to glorify Stalin, its facade is littered with decorative hammers and sickles. Its seventeenth-floor observation deck gives great views of the city (charge). Behind this monument to communism is the wooden **Church of Jesus** (Jēzus baznīca), built in 1822 to replace an earlier house of worship destroyed in the fire that consumed Riga's suburbs a decade earlier. Its unusual octagonal shape was designed to fit the square's limited space.

At the corner of Gogoļa and Dzirnavu streets are the reconstructed ruins of the **Great Choral Synagogue** (Die Greise Hor Shul), which was set ablaze on 4 July 1941 with hundreds of Jewish Lithuanian refugees inside. A memorial stone and a menorah mark

Great Choral Synagogue memorial

the spot of the atrocity. The area around Ludzas iela was part of a ghetto created by the Nazis.

THE LEFT BANK

HIGHLIGHTS

» Latvian Railway History Museum, see page 75
» Riga Aviation Museum, see page 75
» Victory Park, see page 76

The left bank (Pārdaugava) of the River Daugava is home to both apartment blocks and heavy industry. Its working-class neighbourhoods are full of renovated historic nineteenth-century wooden houses, charming churches, decaying Art Nouveau masterpieces and ultra-modern buildings, including the sleek **National Library of Latvia** (www.lnb.lv; guided tours on request) resembling a glass hill. Also known as the Castle of Light, it was designed by the famous Latvian architect Gunārs Birkerts.

The building that houses the **Latvian Railway History Museum** (Latvijas dzelzceļa muzejs; www.railwaymuseum.lv) was a repair workshop for trains in the nineteenth century. Today it contains a variety of exhibits, from engineers' overalls and black-and-white photographs to old wagons and tools used by railway workers. Locomotives and historic carriages on the tracks outside will impress trainspotters. The museum has also become a popular venue for concerts.

On exiting the airport terminal head left towards the cargo buildings to find the **Riga Aviation Museum** (Rīgas aviācijas muzejs; http://airmuseum.lv). Cold War historians and spy novel enthusiasts shouldn't pass up an opportunity to acquaint

---

MIDSUMMER CELEBRATIONS

While Christmas and Easter often top the list of favourite national holidays for many countries, Midsummer's Eve is the most anticipated celebration of the year in Latvia. This ancient pagan fertility festival marks the longest day of the year, and its passing is observed across the country on 23–24 June. All the nation's urban centres empty as cars decorated with oak leaves head for the countryside laden with food and drink. Rural hosts greet their guests with beer, caraway-seed cheese and a song, but the new arrivals aren't able to join the fun until they sing something in return. During the course of the evening, young couples are encouraged to forage through the forest for the fabled fern flower that only blooms on Midsummer. Of course, ferns don't blossom, but it's a charming euphemism for the fertility part of the festivities. Revellers also jump over the bonfire three times for good luck and no one is allowed to sleep until sunrise.

Riga Aviation Museum

themselves with the rusting examples of some of the Soviet Union's finest and most unusual aircraft.

VICTORY PARK

Just over the river is a park with a controversial monument dedicated to the victory over Nazi Germany and the so-called 'liberation' of Latvia. **Victory Park** (Uzvaras parks) is still a popular rallying point for leftists and pensioners on important Soviet anniversary days, yet Latvians view it as a symbol of the loss of their sovereignty and the occupation of their nation by a foreign power. Indeed, a small group of ultranationalists even tried to liberate Riga from its presence with sticks of dynamite. They were unsuccessful. Below the soaring pedestal that supports golden communist stars, Russian-speaking couples lay flowers on their wedding day.

OUTLYING AREAS

HIGHLIGHTS

» Brothers' Cemetery, see page 77
» Forest Park (Mežaparks), see page 78
» The Ethnographic Open-Air Museum of Latvia, see page 79
» Riga Motor Museum, see page 80
» Salaspils Concentration Camp Memorial, see page 80

Once you leave Old Riga and the city centre, the sites worth seeing become fewer and farther between, but the following buildings, parks, museums and monuments are all worth the effort and the inexpensive tram, trolleybus or cab ride.

INTERESTING CEMETERIES

Construction of **Brothers' Cemetery** (Brāļu kapi), dedicated to Latvia's fallen heroes who fought for independence between 1915 and 1920, began in 1924 and was completed in 1936. Among its most impressive features are the sombre statues of soldiers, heads bowed, the eternal flame and Mother Latvia overseeing the entire scene. To reach the cemetery, it's best to take tram route number 11 from Barona.

Latvian Song and Dance Festival

Riga National Zoo

There are a few other interesting cemeteries worth visiting along the way. The **Great Cemetery** (Lielie kapi) was opened in the late eighteenth century and contains the graves of Krišjānis Barons and other famous Latvians. Sadly, most of its artistically significant monuments were shipped to other parts of the USSR after the war to be used by the families of Soviet functionaries. Just across the street next to the tiny Orthodox church is the **Pokrov Cemetery** (Pokrova kapi) with gravestones bearing the epitaphs of prominent tsarist bureaucrats. A small plot of land is also dedicated to Red Army soldiers who were killed in the area during World War II. Further along the tram route is the city's largest final resting place, the **Forest Cemetery** (Meža kapi), which is still used today.

FOREST PARK (MEŽAPARKS)

By the late nineteenth century, Riga's elite had had enough of the city's overcrowded streets and decided to create a park far from the noise and grime of the centre where they could relax in the bosom of nature. Kaiser Park, as it was originally known, was one of Europe's first garden cities, where only summer cottages and entertainment complexes were allowed to be built. Many of those magnificent wooden houses have now been restored and this green section of Riga now commands the city's highest real estate prices.

Forest Park is also home to the **Song Festival Grounds** (Lielā estrāde) where tens of thousands of performers and spectators gather every five years for this monumental undertaking. The **Riga National Zoo** (Rīgas zooloģiskais dārzs; http://rigazoo.lv) is popular with families, though its cramped enclosures and downtrodden air are likely to be at odds with Western sensibilities.

THE ETHNOGRAPHIC OPEN–AIR MUSEUM OF LATVIA

A twenty-minute trip on Bus No. 1 from Tērbatas will transport you to the rural countryside of nineteenth-century Latvia. Explore over 100 hectares (247 acres) of life as it used to be in peasant villages and seaside fishing communities. Established in 1924,

The Ethnographic Open-Air Museum

the **Ethnographic Open-Air Museum of Latvia ❶** (Latvijas etnogrāfiskais brīvdabas muzejs; www.brivdabasmuzejs.lv) is one of the oldest of its kind in Europe and also one of the most impressive. Its architects scoured the agrarian landscape of the nation in search of priceless examples of typical wooden homes, barns, stables, shops, churches and windmills and had them taken apart and painstakingly reassembled on the shores of Lake Jugla. Weavers, blacksmiths, beekeepers and various craftspeople go about their business here in authentic costumes and sell their wares to the delight of all who come. During the summer it hosts a variety of folklore concerts and craft markets too, as well as Midsummer's Eve celebrations (see page 75).

RIGA MOTOR MUSEUM

In the wilds of nine-storey Soviet concrete housing estates in the suburbs, you can view the country's best display of antique cars, motorcycles and military vehicles at the **Riga Motor Museum** (Rīgas motormuzejs; www.motormuzejs.lv). Vintage Rolls-Royces are lined up next to BMWs and Mercedes, not to mention Latvian automobiles produced in the 1920s and 1930s. Among the museum's most impressive exhibits are the cars used by the Soviet elite, including specially designed limousines.

SALASPILS CONCENTRATION CAMP MEMORIAL

Just outside Riga city limits is the sleepy town of Salaspils, which has the dubious distinction of being the scene of one of the twentieth century's most barbaric crimes against humanity. Hidden beyond the pines of its forest is the site of a former Nazi concentration camp, 'Kurtenhof', where more than 100,000 Jews, Latvians, Estonians, Lithuanians, Poles and nearly a dozen other ethnic groups were exterminated. A megalithic concrete structure, which now serves as the gate to the camp and also houses a small exhibit dedicated to the site, is inscribed with the words, 'Beyond this gate the earth moans'. Visitors can view the foundations of some of the prisoners' barracks and the haunting sculptures symbolising the suffering of the camp's victims.

DAY TRIPS

HIGHLIGHTS

- Jūrmala, see page 82
- Sigulda, see page 85
- Bauska region, see page 89

The proud inhabitants of the countryside will be the first to tell you that Riga isn't Latvia. Away from the luxury cars, trendy cafés and

The popular beach at Jūrmala

LAND OF STORKS

If babies come from storks, where to do storks come from? The answer is Latvia. While the number of storks in Europe on the whole is in steady decline, their numbers in Latvia have increased dramatically. Many nations in Western Europe and Scandinavia are now completely lacking in these noble birds, but Latvia has nearly 10,000 pairs of nesting storks, or one pair for every 250 people.

Latvia is also home to the rare black stork, which, unlike its white cousin that often chooses chimneys as nesting platforms, is very shy and only nests in uninhabited areas of the country-side. If the black stork detects the presence of humans, it often abandons its nest.

Latvians have always revered storks and they encourage these large birds to nest on their property by erecting special poles for their huge nests, which often reach 1m (3ft) in diameter. The birds are thought to bring luck, to protect the home and bring fertility. Just drive out of Riga's city limits in nearly any direction in the summer and you're likely to see them. The storks then head back to Africa before the harsh Latvian winter arrives.

designer shops of the city that supports over a third of the nation's population are several historic towns that have yet to shed their traditional lifestyles for the trappings of modern living. Ancient crusader castles, health spas, over 500km (310 miles) of pristine beaches, and hundreds of nature trails for hikers are only a short day trip from the capital city. All of the following destinations are easily accessible by hired car, public transport or organised tour.

JŪRMALA

This loose federation of a dozen small towns spread over nearly 20km (12 miles) of white-sand beaches has long been a favourite summer retreat for Riga's citizens. From its inception as a holiday destination in the nineteenth century, when bathing hours for men and women were strictly regulated to prevent the unseemly commingling of the sexes, to its heyday in the 1930s, when seasonal cottages were built nearly every day, **Jūrmala** , with little more than its beauty and proximity to the sea, has never lost its allure. In fact, during the Soviet era this narrow peninsula jutting out into the Baltic became one of the USSR's most popular resorts, enticing more than six million hard-working proletarians to its shores each year. However, this boom time, in which development went largely unregulated, left parts of this unique landscape scarred with crumbling communist edifices. Many of the current entrepreneurs in the area have also failed to shed their old mindset, so service can often fall short of Western expectations.

But Jūrmala's draw has always been its excellent beaches sheltered by pine forests and sand dunes. In recent years standards have

Villas in Jūrmala

NOTES

Below the castle complex is a series of caves, including the largest in the Baltics, Gutmanis Cave (Gūtmaņa ala), which measures nearly 19m (62ft) deep, 12m (40ft) wide and 10m (33ft) high. Because it is thought to be the place where the Turaida Rose met her end, lovers have left their inscriptions in its sandstone walls since the seventeenth century, many of which are still visible.

---

improved so dramatically as to warrant the prestigious European blue flags that guarantee essential services such as sanitation, changing rooms, lifeguards and medical teams on call. Beer gardens have also sprouted up like mushrooms to meet the demands of thirsty holidaymakers. During the few hot summer months that Latvia experiences, you can expect beaches teeming with people sunbathing, playing football and parading along the sand.

Jūrmala is also home to dozens of spa hotels that offer mud baths and scores of other health treatments often used by German and Finnish pensioners who can't afford such luxuries in their own countries. The urban centres provide top-notch restaurants and nightlife as well as excellent examples of wooden Art Nouveau buildings, not least of which is the **Dubulti Lutheran Church** (Dubultu luterāņu baznīca), whose towering steeple can be seen from a great distance. Those interested in literature can visit the **Rainis and Aspazija Memorial Summer Cottage** (Raiņa un Aspazijas vasarnīca; http://memorialiemuzeji.lv) and see where two of Latvia's most famous writers lived and worked. The library has a collection of more than seven thousand books in eleven languages. A casual stroll down the main pedestrian street of Jomas iela in Majori will afford every visitor with countless opportunities to eat, drink and shop.

One of Latvia's best nature reserves is located at the far west end of Jūrmala. **Ķemeri National Park** (Ķemeru Nacionālais parks) has wetlands, marshes, swamps and raised bogs that have all but disappeared in Western Europe. Nature trails and an observation tower allow visitors to explore the park's 43 hectares (106 acres) and see a variety of animals, including wild boar, elk, deer, wolves and rare birds.

Trains depart for Jūrmala from Riga Central Station every half hour during the summer, and the trip to its largest town, Majori, takes around forty minutes.

SIGULDA

Liv tribesmen, who had settled in the Gauja River region around a thousand years ago, built a wooden fortress high above the valley, but in 1207 it was destroyed by the Brotherhood of the Sword and replaced by a new stone castle. A small town, referred to by

View from Turaida Castle

Cable car in the Gauja valley

the crusaders as Siegewald, flourished at the foot of the new fortress and before long it included churches and even new castles. The fortunes of **Sigulda** ❸ changed when it was overrun twice by Russian troops in the Great Livonian War (1558–82), causing extensive damage. It suffered most, however, during the Polish–Swedish War (1600–29) when its fortifications were destroyed and the ensuing plague ravaged its population.

Sigulda did not recover until the nineteenth century with the opening of the Riga–Pskov railway. Its romantic castle ruins, ancient churches and picturesque valley soon became major tourist attractions earning its hilly, forest-covered terrain the nickname 'Latvia's Switzerland'. Today, Sigulda enjoys the country's most developed tourism infrastructure with the same proven sights, as well as new activities such as nature hikes on marked trails, rafting and canoeing trips on the river, rides down a bobsleigh track and bungee jumping from a cable car above the valley. Sigulda is about an hour's ride by train from Riga.

Sigulda's most striking attraction is the **Turaida Museum Reserve** ❹ (Turaidas muzejrezervāts; www.turaida-muzejs.lv), which offers several noteworthy historical sites, the most obvious being the partially reconstructed brick **Turaida Castle** (Turaidas pils), built in 1214. Archaeological excavations are continuing, but visitors can view the small museum dedicated to the castle and the Liv tribes that once lived in the area. The castle tower offers excellent views of the valley. Outside the castle grounds is one of the oldest wooden churches in Latvia, built in 1750.

Next to the church, beside a giant linden tree, you can see the grave of Maija (1601–20), the **Turaida Rose** (Turaidas Roze). Legend has it that a clerk who lived in the castle discovered a young girl on a battlefield among the dead and dying. She grew up to become a beautiful woman and, despite the interest displayed by the local gentry, fell in love with a commoner who tended the castle gardens. A Polish soldier was entirely enamoured with the girl and asked her hand in marriage, but she refused. Furious, the man and another soldier lured her to a nearby cave and attempted to force her to engage with him. To protect herself, she offered the man a gift of a scarf that

Bauska Castle

Krimulda Castle

could supposedly protect its wearer from harm. As proof of its 'magical' qualities she asked the soldier to try to cut her with his sword. To his horror, he lopped her head off. Today, newlyweds leave flowers at her grave in the hope of attaining the same everlasting (though one-sided it must be added) love. Curiously, medieval records were found that included an account of a woman named Maija who was murdered in the Gutmanis Cave, which may prove that the legend is at least partially based on fact. Beyond the grave is **Folk Song Hill** (Dainu kalns), which is a sculpture park with figures representing various aspects of Latvian folklore and mythology.

Not far from the cable car that leads to the Sigulda city centre are the ruins of the **Krimulda Castle** (Krimuldas pils). Not much remains of the fortress, built in 1312, and it is seldom seen by tourists, but it's worth a visit, especially if you have time to spare while waiting for the next cable car.

The **Sigulda Castle** ❺ (Siguldas pils) is located on the other side of the valley. Its most impressive features, apart from its location, are the tower of the grand gate and the Gothic windows of the chapel. Sigulda's first castle was abandoned after its destruction in the seventeenth century, but a new **manor house** was built next to it, which now houses the city council and a restaurant. All 1.2km (¾ mile) of the **Sigulda Bobsleigh Track** (Siguldas bobslejtrase; www.

bobtrase.lv) are located next to the railway station and guarantee a unique experience for anyone brave enough to take a ride down.

BAUSKA REGION

Although the town of Bauska has little to offer apart from its impressive castle ruins, two magnificent palaces are located within 10km (6 miles) of the city and all three attractions can be incorporated into a day trip from Riga. Construction of **Bauska Castle** (Bauskas pils; www.bauskaspils.lv) began in 1443 as yet another fortress of the Livonian Order. Later it became the residence of the royal family of the Duchy of Courland. Built on a hill above the confluence of two rivers, its ramparts, deep moat, five towers and 4m (13ft) thick walls were still not enough to prevent its partial

Rundāle Palace

destruction during the Great Northern War (1700–21) between Russia and Sweden. Today its well-preserved ruins are no less impressive. Inside are a small museum and an observation tower.

The German barons left behind hundreds of manors and estates across Latvia, but none as grand as **Rundāle Palace** ❻ (Rundāles pils; http://rundale.net). Latvia's most opulent building was the brain-child of Bartolomeo Rastrelli (1700–71), who would later design the Winter Palace in St Petersburg, one-time residence of the tsars and current home of the Hermitage Museum. Rundāle Palace was built between 1736 and 1740, as a residence for Duke Ernst Johann von Biron of Courland (1690–1772). The duke was a favourite of Tsarina Anna (1693–1740), but was stripped of his title on her death, only to return in 1765 after Catherine the Great assumed the throne of

Mežotne Palace

Russia. The palace is the best example of baroque architecture in Latvia and, although it suffered during the wars that ravaged the region, many of its finest attributes have survived. After being issued felt slippers to avoid disturbing the delicate parquet floors, visitors can view a few of the original 138 rooms, including the Gold and White Representation Halls, the Duchess' Boudoir and the Duke's apartments. An exhibit featuring European and East Asian art and other historic treasures is open to the public, as is the French

Sigulda Bobsleigh Track

garden and an exhibit dedicated to priceless religious artefacts saved by Latvians from imminent destruction at the hands of the Soviets.

Mežotne Palace (Mežotnes pils; www.mezotnepalace.com) has been completely renovated and is currently used as a hotel, although it is open to the public for tours. It was completed in 1802 and used to belong to Charlotte von Lieven, a close friend of Catherine the Great. Unfortunately, the palace was gutted several times by various invading troops. The graves in the English garden of seven Russian soldiers who held off a German assault here in 1915, bear witness to this violent history.

Its location on the River Lielupe makes it a great place for a picnic, but those who would prefer to live like royalty can rent a room in the palace for the night and soak up the Neoclassical atmosphere first-hand.

The opulent Opera House

Things to do

From arts and cultural events to a thriving nightlife and rich shopping scene, Riga has no shortage of things to do. Lose yourself among the amber stalls of Old Riga or take in a world-class ballet performance at the city's beautifully restored nineteenth-century Opera House. Duck into a moodily lit club for a taste of whisky and the delta blues or join the crowds at a summer beer garden and order a local brew. Whatever your jam, Riga has something for everyone.

CULTURE

With more than a million folk songs to choose from, Latvians are never short of words to sing, and their collective voice for recent independence was dubbed the 'Singing Revolution'. Similarly, locals have the utmost respect for music, and the result is a vibrant cultural scene. Riga is, after all, the birthplace of classical musician Gidon Kremer, actor and choreographer Mikhail Baryshnikov and film director Sergei Eisenstein.

CLASSICAL MUSIC AND OPERA

With such native sons as Baryshnikov and Alexander Gudunov, it's no surprise that Riga's ballet and opera draw crowds from around Europe. However, what's most surprising to visitors are the low prices for performances and the stunning opulence of the **National Opera House** (Aspazijas bulvāris 3; www.

NOTES

The Latvian Song and Dance Festival has been held roughly every five years since 1873 and its highlight is the final concert during which hundreds of choirs from around the country sing together in front of tens of thousands of spectators who often join in on the most popular songs. They take place approximately every five years.

Small Guild hosts music concerts

opera.lv), which is decorated with gilded ceilings, crystal chandeliers and priceless works of art. The **Great Guild** (Amatu 6) is home to the Latvian Philharmonic Orchestra, while the **Small Guild** (Amatu 3/5; http://mazagilde.lv) across the street often hosts chamber music concerts and special events. No trip to Riga is complete without experiencing an organ concert in the Baltic's largest house of worship, **Dome Cathedral** (Doma laukums 1; www.doms.lv). World-class talent from around the globe often waive their charges just for the opportunity to play on the magnificent organ, which is one of the world's largest, with 6718 pipes. Most major rock and pop concerts are held at **Arena Riga** (Skanstes 21; www.arenariga.com). For cultural events favoured by a young local crowd, the lively **Kaņepes Kultūras centrs** (Skolas iela 15; https://kanepes.lv) runs a wide programme from music to film, live performances to literary readings.

NIGHTLIFE

In a northern city like Riga, the long summer days prevent any temptation to retreat to your hotel, while winter's dark afternoons mean you don't need an excuse to begin early. Trendy cocktail bars, chic clubs, 24hr casinos and down-to-earth pubs occupy nearly every street corner in Riga.

For a cosy, dimly lit atmosphere and premium cocktails, often poured by famous visiting mixologists, head to **Cloud Nine** (Strēlnieku iela 1B; https://cloudnine.lv). The popular **B-Bar**, next to the Dome Cathedral (Doma laukums 2; www.bbars.lv), has live DJ sets and dancing at the weekends. On the top of Galleria Riga, **Herbary** (Dzirnavu iela 67; https://www.herbary.lv) is a glass-house-style rooftop bar pairing fine cocktails (including excellent non-alcoholic options) and city views, best taken in at sunset. For Nordic-inspired cocktails and a young cool crowd, **Gimlet** is a basement bar with a jazzy soundtrack and locally foraged herbal tinctures. The **Royal Casino** (www.royalcasino.lv) is a huge spa, hotel, restaurant and casino complex open 24 hours; Latvian law requires that you register your passport at the door.

Summer evenings are perfect for al fresco entertainment

SHOPPING

From streetside stalls to inventive concept stores, independent art galleries and a huge market, Riga has shopping to suit every taste. Local handicrafts and foodie products such as sweets make excellent souvenirs and gifts. Most shops accept major credit cards, but look for stickers at the entrance or on the cash register to be sure.

WHERE TO SHOP

There is no specific shopping district in Riga. Most souvenir and local handicraft shops as well as art galleries can be found in the old city and what seems an endless queue of amber stalls awaits you on Līvu Square, Skārņu and Vaļņu iela. Fashion and design is more commonly found in the city centre, especially on K. Barona, Brīvības and Tērbatas streets. Antiques shops are dotted all over the city and usually specialise in porcelain, paintings, icons and a variety of memorabilia from the Soviet era.

Amber stalls

Even if you don't want to spend any money, the Central Market (see page 72) is well worth a visit. Dairy, meat, fresh produce and seafood are sold in four of the five pavilions that once served as Zeppelin hangars during World War I. Here, you will be treated to a colourful scene that has remained largely unchanged since the market first opened in the 1930s. Expect mounds of sauerkraut, barrels of pickled cucumbers and an abundance of local honey, jams, jellies and preserves. Vendors entice passersby with their best cuts of meat or samples of fresh cheese, while butchers with arms like tree trunks skilfully dissect livestock. The stalls spill out onto the pavement behind the buildings where anything from cheap garments to CDs are sold.

WHAT TO BUY

Since ancient times, the polished chunks of petrified tree sap that wash up on the shores of the Baltic Sea have been a useful commodity to the region's inhabitants and their diverse trading partners. **Amber** is still the most popular souvenir bought in Latvia and is sold in every tourist shop or outdoor stall. It comes in various sizes, in colours ranging from light yellow to dark brown and can even be found with prehistoric flora and insects trapped inside. Avoid the shady amber touts who present their dubious wares from a plastic bag. **Silver** rings, bracelets and earrings based on ancient Baltic designs and motifs are also popular examples of local decorative jewellery. The braided, rope-like ring worn by most Latvians is called a *Nameja gredzens*. It symbolises national unity and is named after a famous thirteenth-century tribal chieftain who refused to submit to the invading German crusaders.

Many traditional Latvian handicrafts also make practical gifts or souvenirs and can often be a unique addition to your home's interior design. Latvia is famous for its **linen** products, most notably

⌐ MEDICINAL PURPOSES ¬

Rīgas Melnais Balzams or Riga Black Balsam is perhaps one of the best souvenirs you can buy in Latvia. It has been produced in Latvia since 1752 when a pharmacist began marketing his concoction of 25 herbs, flowers, berries and other secret ingredients as an elixir. Given the fact that it also has an alcohol content of 45 percent and contains wormwood, the substance that gives absinthe its kick, it's no wonder that people forgot about their pain, at least for an hour or two. Bottled in brown ceramic jugs, it's also an attractive gift to inflict on your friends. Although Latvians still drink the black bitter neat, especially as a hangover cure, most locals combine it with coffee, cola or fruit juice. Hot blackcurrant nectar with a shot of Balzams is one of Riga's most popular winter cocktails, although some prefer the Riga Souvenir – Balzams mixed with local sparkling wine. Enjoy the national drink at your own risk.

tablecloths, which are available in many different styles, some with simple Latvian symbols and patterns, others dyed in various colours for more modern tastes. Hand-woven **blankets** coloured with only natural dyes, hand-carved **wooden toys**, wicker baskets and stunning glazed **ceramics** are also on offer at most souvenir shops. An excellent place to buy Latvian crafts, fashion by local designers as well as food and drink is the bustling Kalnciema fair held at the corner of Melnsila and Kalnciema streets every Saturday from 10am–4pm. Off the tourist trail, Galerija Istaba (Krišjāņa Barona iela 31B) is an art gallery, design shop and restaurant in one. Walls are hung with artwork from that month's exhibition while Latvian-made items, from jewellery to clothes, fill the shelves.

Riga's **antiques shops** usually offer an eclectic collection of knick-knacks, porcelain statues and tableware, paintings and furniture. Many also specialise in Russian religious icons, but bear in mind that an icon's journey from a local chapel to a shop may not have been sanctioned by its parishioners or the government. Ask for documentation if the icon's history is unclear. Soviet memorabilia, including uniforms, medals, coins and busts of Lenin, are also widely available, as are silver spoons from tsarist times. Tourists are also often surprised by the number of antique books that are available in German and Russian – the languages of the old empire. Opposite the Art Nouveau Centre, Otto Racens is a charming shop named after owner Zigita Lavrinovicha's grandfather. Zigita, a one-time wardrobe mistress at the Latvian National Opera, has drawn upon her designer-collector credentials to curate a beautiful display of vintage crockery and glassware, hand-stitched Latvian mittens and her own fashion designs.

Music always makes a good gift and Riga's pedigree as home to Richard Wagner and Eurovision superstar band Brainstorm (Prāta

Colourful local knits

Vētra) is reason enough to buy a local CD. The Latvian Folk Music Collection series produced by the Upe Recording Studio is a good place to start. Each CD in the series is based on a theme such as Latvian dances, songs about war, and songs about beer. The disc of Latvian lullabies is a perfect present for parents with small children. Albums by Skandinieki and Iļǵi are also recommended.

Finally, **local food** is always a good memento. Laima chocolates have been made in Riga since the early twentieth century and are simply delicious, not to mention cheap. Black and rye breads are baked according to traditional recipes and never use food colouring to achieve their golden brown hues. Latvians judge honey the way the French judge a good wine, and prices vary widely depending on what flowers the bees visited to collect their pollen.

Homewares by Latvian designers make good gifts

Caraway-seed cheese served at Midsummer festivities is as Latvian a food as they come, but is not everyone's cup of tea, so you may wish to taste a free sample at the market before buying a large quantity. Definitely an acquired taste are miniature lamprey eels cooked in their own juices and then tinned for export.

Bobsleigh run at Sigulda

SPORTS

Latvians love sports, and not just the ones that they're good at. You'll often find as many locals as expatriates watching English Premiership football at sports bars and your average thirty-something can usually spout off enough statistics about their favourite Formula 1 driver to make you wonder if they have a vested interest in Williams or Ferrari.

ICE HOCKEY

Ice hockey is a national obsession and Latvians worship their hip-checking heroes, especially the ones that play in the National Hockey League (NHL). Each year at the beginning of May businesses close early and the citizens of Riga head out to their favourite pubs to watch their team strive for glory in the World Hockey Championship. A victory often leads to gatherings of hundreds of fans who parade about the city shouting slogans and singing songs, often ending their wanderings at the embassy of their vanquished foes. A new arena was built for the hockey champion-ship in 2006, when the Soviet-style Rīgas Sporta Pils was finally retired. In 2007, the Russian Super Hockey League was replaced by the Kontinental Hockey League, which includes a few teams like Dynamo Riga (www.dinamoriga.lv), located beyond the borders of the Russian Federation. Home games are played at Arena Riga.

FOOTBALL

Although it doesn't command the same amount of respect that hockey does, **football** has become increasingly popular, especially since Latvia participated in the Euro 2004 Football Championship in Portugal where they held world-champions Germany to a draw. After winning the Latvian Championship every year since

Residents of the Riga National Zoo

the club's founding in 1991, FC Skonto were finally dislodged from their exalted position in 2005. The team recovered the title in 2010 and finished as runner-up in 2015. However, the club regrettably went bankrupt in 2016. FC Skonto matches in Riga used to be held at the Skonto Stadium (E. Melngaiļa 1a; www.skontofc. com), now the Riga FC club home ground. Riga FC was founded in 2014 and was the Latvian Higher League champion three years running from 2018–2020, and Latvian Cup winners in 2018 and 2023.

Riga is within striking distance of a couple of golf courses

BOBSLEIGH

The historic town of Sigulda, just a short ride from Riga (see page 86), has the only world-class **bobsleigh and luge run** (www. bobtrase.lv) in the former Soviet Union. When professionals aren't training at the difficult run on weekends, an instructor will take you for a quick slide down the mountain year-round at speeds in excess of 125kmh (80mph).

GOLF

If a relaxing round of **golf** is more to your liking, you can choose from an exclusive 18-hole lakeside course (OZO, Mielgrāvja 16; www.ozogolf.lv) owned by the hockey star Sandis Ozoliņš, *Jūrmala*

Lido Leisure Centre

Golf Club & Hotel (Golfa iela 1, Pinki; http://jgch.lv), which offers an 18-hole course, or a less challenging nine-hole course by the airport (Viesturi; www.golfsviesturi.lv).

RIGA FOR CHILDREN

There are only so many churches and historic Art Nouveau buildings that a child can bear before throwing a tantrum. Riga may not be the most child-friendly city in Eastern Europe, but a growing number of restaurateurs have become aware of touristing families and have invested in highchairs for their younger customers. *Vairāk Saules* (Dzirnavu 60; www.vairaksaules.lv) offers a play area for kids to burn off energy while waiting for food. The state **Puppet Theatre** (K. Barona 16/18; www.lelluteatris.lv) is an excellent place for children to spend time with one another and, although the plays are performed in either Latvian or Russian, the plot is generally easy enough to follow and is seldom as interesting as the puppets themselves.

Laima Chocolate Musuem (Miera 22; www.laimasokolades muzejs.lv) offers a tour of Latvia's oldest chocolate and sweets factory, including workshops (advance booking essential) where children can learn how to make chocolate and have a picture beside the famous Laima clock – the symbol of love, joy and new beginnings.

The **Latvian Open-Air Ethnographic Museum** (Brīvības gatve 440; tel: 6799 45 15; see page 80) provides 100 hectares (247 acres) of rural life presented the way it used to be during the nineteenth century. Blacksmiths operate the bellows and forge horseshoes and other iron souvenirs, beekeepers extract honey for tourists to taste, and horseriding can also be arranged. The **Museum of Natural History** (see page 67) is also a good option for children and indeed many school groups often wander its hallways. Ancient fossils, mounted taxidermic wonders, and all manner of creepy-crawly insects are on display for any curious child to admire.

At the **Zinoo Science and Curiosity Center** (Dzirnavu 67, Gallerija Rīga, 5th floor; www.zinoo.lv) the interactive exhibits

Laima Chocolate Museum

Pottery class at the Latvian Open-Air Ethnographic Museum

encourage children to explore the secrets of science with the slanting room, Tesla coil or levitating water being major attractions.

The **Riga National Zoo** (see page 79) is also a popular choice with families. Recent improvements have made the Soviet-era exhibitions much more palatable to the Western tourist. A quick tram ride from the centre will bring you in sight of lions, leopards, musk oxen, alligators and other beasts from around the globe.

In operation for over a hundred years, the **Riga Circus** (Merķeļa 4; www.cirks.lv) is always a hit with kids and has thankfully phased out the use of wild animals in its performances, following a request from the Ministry of Culture.

Līvu Akvaparks **water park** (Lielupe, Vienības gatve 36; www.akvaparks.lv) offers six water slides, a wave pool, children's pool, a tubing river and various other attractions guaranteed to keep the kids engaged for several hours. The 'Tornado' tube is one of the biggest in the world. No trip to Riga would be complete without a short trip to the kitschy **Lido Leisure Centre** (Krasta 76; www. lido.lv). The complex's main attraction is a huge log cabin, with three floors of Latvian restaurants, beer halls with live music, and a supervised children's room with interactive games and activities. Outside is an **amusement park**, which offers slides, games, pony rides, in-line skating and ice-skating in winter.

CALENDAR OF EVENTS

February–March The International Bach Chamber Music festival (www.music.lv) draws musicians from all over Europe.

April The International Baltic Ballet Festival (www.ballet-festival.lv) features the best performers from the Baltic Sea region.

June (first weekend) A crafts fair at the Ethnographic Museum.

22 June Annual Dome Square crafts fair.

23–24 June Midsummer's Eve. Latvia's favourite national holiday is celebrated on the actual date and never moved to the closest week-end for the sake of convenience. The pagan fertility celebrations con-sist of singing, dancing, lots of beer and bonfires in the countryside.

June Past stars at the two-week Riga Opera Festival include Warren Mok and Inese Galante (www.opera.lv).

July *Rīgas Ritmi* Rhythmic Music Festival. Contemporary jazz stars (international and domestic) take part in this annual festival (www. rigasritmi.lv), which now also has winter and spring concert sessions.

August–September Musicians from around the Baltic and Europe converge at the Riga Sacred Music Festival each year to play reli-gious music, especially at the Dome Cathedral. The annual autumn harvest festival is celebrated on the last Saturday of September in Old Riga.

September–October *Homo Novus* International Festival of Contemporary Theatre, dating back to 1995.

December Christmas concerts and crafts market on Dome Square.

Food and drink

All of Latvia's occupiers over the years – from the Swedes to the Germans to the Russians – have left their mark on the nation's cuisine. Traditionally, peasant food was hearty and humble, drawing on a handful of chief ingredients: pork, potatoes, cabbage. Kitchens have evolved since independence and today menus are inventive and innovative, without losing sight of the country's cultural roots. A new generation of chefs are elevating Latvian dishes with culinary influences and cooking techniques from around the globe. What's more, Latvia's inaugural Michelin guide was released in 2024, featuring 26 restaurants spread across the country; nineteen of which are in the capital. *Max Cekot Kitchen* was the first to be awarded a Michelin star, paving the way for more chefs to gain international recognition.

Hearty, humble Latvian food

Curiously, despite Riga's location on the Baltic Sea in northern Europe, there is a puzzling absence of fresh seafood offerings yet a profusion of Armenian cuisine. Food from the Caucasus Mountains can be explained by the arrival of Armenian refugees fleeing a devastating earthquake in 1988, but the absence of crab, lobster, oysters and other sea creatures remains a mystery. These days, there is a greater diversity in restaurants in Riga, with excellent

---

TOP TIPPLES

Most Latvians enjoy a good drink, and beer is the undisputed favourite in Old Riga during summer. Although Aldaris, which makes several different varieties of beer, has the largest market share, several smaller breweries have also gained in popularity, not least of which northern Europe's oldest brewery, Cēsu Alus, which has been in operation since 1590. Užavas, Tērvetes, Piebalgas, Bauskas and Valmiermuiža are more traditional beers brewed in smaller quantities and well worth a try. Despite the country's long brewing traditions, spirits still reign supreme in Latvia. Latvijas Balzams produces dozens of different vodkas, brandies, whiskies and flavoured liqueurs, but its most famous product is the herbal bitter Rīgas Melnais Balzams, Riga Black Balsam.

Japanese, Italian and Indian ventures springing up across the streets. Vegetarians won't struggle like they would have just five years ago, but they should be specific when ordering to ensure that a garden salad isn't topped with bacon, or a supposedly meatless soup isn't infused with chunks of ham.

TOP 10 FOODS TO TRY

1. BORSCHT (AUKSTĀ ZUPA)

A refreshing cold soup with a deep pink, purply colour, *aukstā zupa* is made with beets, cucumbers, kefir, hard-boiled eggs and milk sausage; the soup is then topped with various greens, such as dill and scallions. It is usually served with a few slices of dark bread on the side. The dish is seasonal and best enjoyed alfresco on a hot summer's day.

2. BLOOD SAUSAGE (ASINSDESA)

Asinsdesa, or blood sausage, is similar to the Scottish speciality black pudding. Made from pork blood and various fillers like

┌─ **NOTES** ──────────

Always look each of your
fellow drinkers in the eye
when clinking beer mugs
at a bar with locals. You can
also impress Latvians by say-
ing *priekā!*, which is Latvian
for 'Cheers!'.

barley, oatmeal and speck, this hearty sausage encased in a natural intestine skin is usually eaten in the winter. The standard Latvian variant is *'putraimu desa'*, which translates literally as 'groat sausage' as the recipe includes barley groats (or hulled barley). It is fried and then eaten usually with marinated pumpkin, cucumbers and lingonberry or wild cranberry jam, or with grated horseradish. It's served as either a main or side dish.

3. PĪRĀGI AND OTHER SPECIALITIES

Being a nation of farmers for so many years, Latvia's national foods are, to put it mildly, rustic in nature. *Pīrāgi* are small pastry buns traditionally, although not exclusively, filled with chopped ham and onions. Others are stuffed with minced meat, cheese and even sauerkraut and are available in most cheap cafés. A bowl of boiled grey peas fried with bacon and onions is also a favourite Latvian treat and is often topped with kefīr, a dairy drink similar to yoghurt. Available at most traditional Latvian restaurants, peas are also eaten at Christmas and New Year's Eve to bring good luck in the coming year. Latvians also pride themselves on a wide variety of local sausages, which, when compared to German bratwurst or knackwurst, just don't cut the mustard. However, the thin *med-nieku desiņas*, or hunters' sausages, are by far the most popular type and definitely worth a try.

4. LOCAL CHEESE

Cottage cheese (or *biezpiens*, variously known as curds, quark or farmers' cheese) is eaten daily in Latvia, often with sour cream, dill, parsley, cucumber or radish on rye bread. Sometimes it's combined with flour, sugar and egg, and then fried like a pancake (*biezpiena placenisi*). Jāņi cheese (*Jāņu siers*) is equally adored by Latvians, and has its roots in midsummer celebrations, its yellow colour representing the sun. Melted cheese (*kausētais siers*) and smoked cheese (*kūpināts siers*) are just as popular, the latter typically served as a bar snack.

5. RYE BREAD

Rye bread, or *rupjmaize*, is one of the most prominent foods in the Latvian diet. Its main ingredients are rye flour, malt and caraway seeds, which, when combined, give the bread its distinct colour and full-bodied texture. A sweet twist on the classic is rye bread

New Nordic fine dining

Piragi – bacon and onion buns

pudding, where ground rye bread is mixed with dried or fresh fruit, honey and spices; baked; and topped with a dollop of whipped cream.

6. MEATY SNACKS

The Armenian treat *basturma* is a favourite in Riga: paper-thin beef slices that taste like American jerky. A dining experience at a Slavic-style restaurant is never complete without a plate of *salo*, which is flavoured bacon fat sliced into thin strips and rolled into small cones. On occasion, Latvian bars will serve pigs' ears, considered a delicacy by locals.

7. SAUERKRAUT

Although the recipe may vary from family to family, sauerkraut (sour cabbage) is essentially finely shredded cabbage fermented in brine. It's thought to have originated in China thousands of years ago, arriving in Latvia with the Germans. Over time, it has become an intrinsic part of the Latvian cooking repertoire, served as a side dish, condiment or added to soup. At Christmas, it's often sauteed and served as a main with boiled potatoes and pork.

8. GRIĶI (BUCKWHEAT)

Another staple of the Latvian kitchen, *griķi* (buckwheat) is typically eaten at breakfast. Traditionally, it is boiled in water and served unaccompanied except for a sliver of butter or dollop of sour cream and pinch of salt. The buckwheat dish, which some say resembles porridge, is also added to salads or eaten with meat dishes such as *karbonāde* (pork schnitzel) or *karbonāde ar kaulu* (pork chops).

9. DESSERTS

One traditional Latvian dessert that crops up everywhere is *ķīselis*: oat porridge sweetened with seasonal fruit and forest berries. Otherwise, menus concentrate on familiar items like ice cream (*saldējums*), gateau (*torte*) and cakes (*kūkas*). Pancakes (*pankūkas*) come with a variety of fillings, notably *biezpiens* or curd cheese, which is slightly sweetened to achieve a cheesecake-like taste. Tasty little chocolate-coated cubes of *biezpiens* (Kārums is the best-known brand) can be picked up from supermarket chiller cabinets.

10. BLACK BALSAM

Black Balsam has been produced in Latvia since 1752, when a pharmacist began marketing his concoction of 25 herbs, flowers, berries

---

WEEDS AND SEEDS

In the absence of any exotic spices, such as chillies, generations of Latvian mothers and grandmothers have had to make do with what the Baltic's sandy shores can offer to enliven their otherwise bland dishes of pork, cabbage and potatoes. The most ubiquitous of these is dill. The kitchens of all but the finest restaurants in Riga have giant buckets of the green weed, which is liberally applied to any dish, not excluding pizza and pasta. The second offender is caraway seeds, which are called for in nearly every Latvian recipe. They are added to salads and sauerkraut, baked into bread and meatballs and generously sprinkled on roasts of all kinds. Although restaurant staff won't understand why anyone would eat a meal without these weeds and seeds, you can nevertheless order your food *bez dillēm/ķimenēm* (without dill/caraway seeds).

and other secret ingredients as an elixir. Given the fact that it also has an alcohol content of 45 percent and contains wormwood, the substance that gives absinthe its kick, it's no wonder people forgot about their pain, at least for an hour or two. Bottled in brown ceramic jugs, it's also an attractive gift to inflict on your friends. Although Latvians still drink the black bitter neat, especially as a hangover cure, most locals combine it with coffee, cola or fruit juice.

WHERE TO EAT

Many establishments in Riga try to be everything to everyone, often billing themselves as restaurants, clubs, bars and even casinos all in one, so the distinctions between them are often blurred. Some bars serve excellent food worthy of the finest gastronomic institutions in the city, while some restaurants are popular places simply to drink beer. The following is a general explanation of establishments you'll encounter in Riga.

Restorāni (restaurants) seem to occupy nearly every square metre of available space in Old Riga and some of the best areas of the centre. Although most kitchens put their faith in international fare to attract a diverse crowd of patrons, many have dedicated their kitchens to specific cuisines such as Indian, Armenian, Japanese and Korean. Bear in mind that garnishes, bread and even condiments may not be included in the price of a meal and a ten percent gratuity may be automatically added, so check the bill.

Locals often take comfort in their local *kafejnīcas* (cafés), which offer greasy dishes such as pork chops and other heavy foods guaranteed to clog your arteries. Prices are almost always just short of ridiculously cheap, but menus are rarely in English. Many of these establishments also offer an inexpensive buffet, so you can often just point to whatever you would like to eat or simply pile up your plate yourself.

Krogi (bars) usually offer menus for lunch and dinner and remain open for drinks until midnight and perhaps later, seldom closing before 2am on weekends. Most *alus bāri* (beer bars) are typically located around the railway station, Central Market and other areas with heavy footfall. Craft beer is deeply embedded in local culture, and bars across the capital act as a showcase for Latvian producers. Valmiermuiža (Aristida Briana iela 9A Valdemara Pasaza) in Riga is a good place to try some of these unique brews.

Home-made cheese

TO HELP YOU ORDER...

Could we have a table? **Vai būtu kāds brīvs galds?**

I'd like... **Man lūdzu...**	milk **piens**
The bill, please **Rēķinu, lūdzu**	pepper **pipari**
beer **alus**	potatoes **kartupeļi**
bread **maize**	rice **rīsi**
butter **sviests**	salad **salāti**
coffee **kafija**	salt **sāls**
eggs **olas**	sandwich **sendvičs**
fish **zivs**	soup **zupa**
fruit **augļi**	sugar **cukurs**
ice cream **saldējums**	tea **tēja**
meat **gaļa**	water **ūdens**
menu **ēdienkarte**	wine **vīns**

...AND READ THE MENU

biezzupa stew	**mārrutki** horseradish
burkāni carrots	**menca** cod
cūkgaļa pork	**mērce** sauce
dārzeņi vegetables	**ogas** berries
desa sausage	**pelmeņi** dumplings
eļļa oil	**pupas** beans
etiķis vinegar	**sēnes** mushrooms
foreleg trout	**siers** cheese
garšvielas spices	**sīpols** onion
jēragaļa lamb	**šķiņķis** ham
kāposti cabbage	**šnicele** schnitzel
karbonāde pork chop	**steiks (liellops)** steak (beef)
ķimenes caraway	**teļagaļa** veal
ķiploki garlic	**tītars** turkey
kotletes meatballs	**trusis** rabbit
kūka cake	**vista** chicken
lasis salmon	**zirņi** peas

Places to eat

Each restaurant and café reviewed in this Guide is accompanied by a price category, based on the cost of a three-course meal (or similar) for one.

€€€€€ = over €25
€€€€ = €14–25
€€€ = €10–14
€€ = €7–10
€ = under €7

OLD RIGA

Bon Vivant Mārstaļu 8, www.bonvivant.lv. Riga's only authentic Belgian beer bar and restaurant offers a cosy, rustic atmosphere and a fantastic menu that includes a variety of mussels, giant sausages ordered by the half-metre and specialities like country beef stewed in dark beer. Several delicious brews from the Low Countries are all served in their proper glasses and the staff are friendly. €€€

Folkklubs Ala Pagrabs Peldu 19, www.folkklubs.lv. This popular bar/restaurant specialises in authentic, filling Latvian fare. It's furnished in rustic style: you can either sit at a small wooden table or share a large one with strangers. As many as 27 Latvian draught beers are offered. Live concerts at least five times a week, mostly of Latvian folk music. Really fun venue, and always a good night out. €€

Indian Raja Skārņu 7, www.indianraja.lv. Latvians speak an Indo-European language, but any other similarities with the people of the sub-continent end there, which explains the lack of locals here. *Indian Raja* is, however, full of expatriates and tourists who can't get enough of authentic curries and other traditional Indian dishes in this charming cellar restaurant. €€€

Max Cekot Kitchen Jelgavas iela 42, https://www.maxcekot.com. Set in a red-brick warehouse, Latvia's first Michelin-starred restaurant is helmed by chef-owner Max Cekot. A fourteen-course tasting menu is prepared in front of diners in the open kitchen, and though dishes change with the seasons, the commitment to local, seasonal produce never waivers. Max himself explains each course to patrons, and it's a thoroughly enjoyable experience (though, perhaps not for your wallet). €€€€

Melnie mūki Jāṇa sēta 1 (entrance from Kalēju), www.melniemuki.lv. The former personal chef to Latvia's first post-communist president master-minded this elegant restaurant located in a section of a medieval convent. The choice is so extensive that it could take hours to decide what to eat, but the menu often includes anecdotes about the source of, and inspiration behind, each recipe. Reservations recommended. €€€

Milda Kungu iela 8, https://restoransmilda.lv. Awarded a bib gourmand in Latvia's inaugural Michelin guide, this unassuming restaurant named after the figure atop the Freedom Monument gives a modern spin on classic dishes; try the Latvian grey peas with smoked bacon and sour cream. €€€

Monterosso Vaļņu 9, www.monterosso.lv. Given the fact that this place is often filled with members of the local Italian community, it's fairly safe to say that the cuisine served here meets with their approval. Elegant wood-panelled walls, high ceilings and a general air of old-world opulence awaits, as do pizzas, pastas and main dishes alongside an excellent selection of Italian wines. The house special is *frutti di mare* over black pasta. Delicious pastries are also available at the cappuccino bar open from 10am. €€€€

Rozengrāls Rozena 1, www.rozengrals.lv. Although many restaurants may claim to be authentically medieval, *Rozengrāls* is the real deal: it is located in a thirteenth-century cellar once used by town officials for feasts;

potatoes, tomatoes and other food that wouldn't have been available in medieval Latvia are absent from the menu and the entire staff is dressed in period costume. Local brews and curious drinks concocted from centuries-old recipes are also on offer. €€€€

Shōyu Ausekļa iela 20, https://www.shoyu.lv. Dinky ramen shop churning out incredible bowls of home-made noodles in full-flavoured broths, topped with various fresh ingredients. Also serves a selection of delicious rice bowls. €€€

Snatch Elizabetes iela 39, https://snatch.lv. Cool concrete-walled restaurant popular with a young crowd for its authentic Italian food, excellent cocktails and buzzy soundtrack. Try the rabbit pappardelle with beans. €€€

Soraksans Miesnieku 12, tel: 6722 90 68. This inviting restaurant decorated with paper lanterns was the first of its kind in Riga to offer authentic Korean cuisine at prices that average Latvians could afford, and it's still incredibly popular, drawing in crowds at lunchtime. Kimchi, sushi and bibimbap (rice dish), served in red-hot earthenware bowls, are just some of its specialities. €€

Tam labam būs augt Torņa iela 4, www.3pavari.lv. The name ('What's good will grow') says it all. This trendy restaurant-bar run by three popular chefs – Mārtiņš Sirmais, Ēriks Dreibants and Artūrs Trinkuns – offers some of the best modern Latvian cuisine. Most meals are prepared using slow cooking methods, then served on a paper card or granite slab by the chef himself, who is eager to unveil the culinary secrets behind his creations. The menu is short, seasonal and changes so often that even the most faddy gourmets will be satisfied. €€€€

Zviedru Varti Torņa iela 4–1a, https://zviedruvarti.lv. Next to the Swedish Gate, this family-run venture in a sixteenth-century building offers comforting classics like duck breast with pear and red wine sauce or pork leg with stewed cabbage. €€€€

THE CENTRE

Barents Smilšu iela 3, www.barents.lv. Hotly tipped for a Michelin star, this ambitious restaurant serves a seafood-leaning menu where the dishes are as artfully presented as they are delicious. Standouts include the Norwegian Sea diver scallops, and the venison with seasonal mushrooms and port wine sauce. Expensive but worth the splurge for a fancy occasion. €€€€

Bergs Elizabetes 83/85 (Berga Bazars), www.hotelbergs.lv. Even if the food is delicious, sometimes you simply can't get past the fact that you're eating in a hotel restaurant. *Bergs* is an exception to the rule. Modern, minimalist interior design, impeccable service and an excellent menu of fusion cuisine make it the go-to destination for upmarket dining in Riga. €€€€

COD Tērbatas iela 45, https://www.cod.lv. Contemporary Japanese plates such as sushi, tempura and gyoza, as well as a robata grill; the black cod with sweet miso is a hit. €€€€

Gastronome Krasta 68a, www.mc2.lv. This stylish grill bar offers delicious seafood, from fresh oysters and scallops to steamed mussels and lobster imported from fifteen countries. If you prefer to do the cooking yourself, you can also buy fresh shellfish and seafood from the Gastronome delicatessen located next door. €€€€

Italissimo Baznīcas 27/29, tel: 2656 48 67. Tasty Italian food served in stylish surroundings. Platters of mixed grilled meat and seafood, and the tortellini are worth a try, as are its traditional mouthwatering desserts. The restaurant also offers a decent selection of Italian wines to choose from. A family-friendly place with a separate room for children who can play there with a childminder. €€€

Riviera Dzirnavu 31 (entrance from Antonijas), http://rivierarestorans.lv. Located only a fifteen-minute walk from the Freedom Monument, *Riviera* is a fish lovers' paradise. The abundant choice of classic seafood dishes includes brook trout, pike perch, grilled catfish, mahi-mahi, halibut and many others. The seafood platter is perfect for groups. Meanwhile, carnivores can opt for a choice of prime cuts cooked to perfection on the wood-fired grill. The wine list features more than 250 bottles, mainly from the Mediterranean or New World. €€€€

Vairāk saules Dzirnavu 60, www.vairaksaules.lv. Although the menus and interior of this stylish pizzeria and cocktail bar are reminiscent of chain restaurants, the atmosphere is warm and the staff are incredibly friendly. In addition to pizzas, pastas, pork chops and other mains, a children's menu is on offer, as well as an entire list of dedicated Tyrolean cuisine. €€

Whitehouse Terbatas iela 2, www.vairaksaules.lv. After a shake-up in 2020, former foodie institution *Biblioteka* reopened as *Whitehouse*, with the same coveted outdoor dining terrace and the same fine views of Vērmane Park, but a new chef at the helm. Expect modern European cuisine with an Asian twist, best paired with one of the signature cocktails. €€

FURTHER AFIELD

Lido atpūtas centrs Krasta 76, www.lido.lv. Difficult to describe, the Lido Leisure Centre is a huge log cabin surrounded by an amusement park. Inside is what must be Northern Europe's largest buffet, divided into sections, each easily recognisable by the symbol hanging above it, such as a chicken, a cow, a pig, a potato. Downstairs you can listen to live Latvian bands or try one of the beers brewed on the premises. Table service is available on the top floor for anyone who wants to avoid the crowds. €€

Travel essentials

PRACTICAL INFORMATION

ACCESSIBLE TRAVEL

Riga is a headache for anyone in a wheelchair. Pavements can be rocky, kerbs steep, and many restaurants, cafés, shops and museums are only accessible via cramped, narrow staircases. On the positive side, traffic in the Old Town is restricted, leaving the streets wide open for pedestrian explorers. Although the situation has recently improved as Latvia is bound to meet EU regulations, visitors in wheelchairs will sometimes need to ask numerous, pointed and direct questions about a hotel's facilities to ensure they can be accommodated. The largest and newest hotels are fairly accessible, and almost always have rooms specially equipped for disabled guests. All new buildings and principal museums are equipped with accessible facilities. The number of buses, trams and trolleybuses with essential equipment to aid in boarding is growing, and the major taxi companies also offer cars designed for disabled passengers.

ACCOMMODATION

Quality, affordable accommodation is difficult to find in Riga. Local hoteliers seem to be under the mistaken impression that all Westerners are incredibly wealthy and eager to part with their euros. Some reasonably priced rooms are available, but thrifty travellers should book well in advance of their arrival date, perhaps even months ahead if planning a visit in the summer. For those who don't mind spending over €90 per night, Riga offers a wide range of excellent accommodation from stylish boutique hotels in refurbished medieval buildings to modern suites with private saunas. Breakfast and twelve percent VAT are almost always included in rates, but hotels often charge more for rooms with good views of Old Riga or other major tourist attractions.

Although not recommended during the summer months due to a likely lack of availability, accommodation can also be booked upon arrival at the airport or Riga Information Centre, Rātslaukums 6, tel: 6703 79 00, www.liveriga.com. Booking a room of any price range is seldom a chore during autumn and winter when occupancy rates plummet. In addition to Latvian and Russian, most hotel staff speak English and sometimes German.

Riga has witnessed an unprecedented proliferation of quality youth hostels to accommodate budget travellers. Beds in dorm rooms seldom

cost more than €12 per person.
Riga Old Town Hostel Vaļņu 43, www.rigaoldtownhostel.lv.
Central Hostel E. Birznieka-Upīša 20, www.centralhostel.lv.

A single/double room with bath/shower **Vienvietīgu/
   Divvietīgu numuru ar vannu/dušas kabīni**
What's the rate per night? **Cik maksā par vienu nakti?**
Is breakfast included? **Vai brokastis ir iekļautas cenā?**

AIRPORT

Riga International Airport, known by its code as RIX, is located 13km (8 miles) outside the city centre and is easily accessed by taxi or bus. Substantial investment by the European Bank for Reconstruction and Development has transformed a small concrete block of a building into a shiny glass and metal testament to modernity. In addition to the national airline airBaltic, Riga is served from London by Ryanair, easyJet, Wizz Air and a few charter operators. For more information visit www.riga-airport.com.

A queue of reputable taxis is always available outside and the trip to the city centre takes roughly twenty minutes. City bus No. 22 picks up passengers on the far side of the car park when exiting the arrivals hall. Shuttle minibuses Nos 241 or 322 depart every thirty minutes for the city centre. A ticket (€2 single) can be purchased from the driver, vending machines or the airport's tourist bureau (a single ticket with e-talons rechargeable card costs €1.15). For schedules see www.rdsd.lv.

A Riga Shuttle Bus leaves every thirty minutes (10.30am–7pm) from P1 parking space in front of E gateway doors (a single ticket that can be bought from the driver costs €5).

What bus do I take to the centre? **Ar kādu autobusu man
   jābrauc uz centru?**
How much is the fare to...? **Cik maksā biļete līdz...?**

> Will you tell me when to get off? **Lūdzu pasakiet, kad jāizkāpj.**

APPS

International taxi app Bolt (https://bolt.eu) is available in Riga, as is car-sharing app CityBee (https://citybee.lt), which is useful if you are trying to visit places that are not easily accessible via bus or train. It is also a good idea to download Google Maps for navigating the city and the Rīgas satiksmes app for getting a handle on the public transport system.

BUDGETING FOR YOUR TRIP

Once remarkably cheap compared to Western cities, Riga has become increasingly expensive. Average prices for essentials are as follows:

Airport transfer. Taxis to the city centre cost around €15. The trip to the centre by bus or minibus will cost between €1.15–€5.

Public transport. An e-talon rechargeable card can be bought from ticket offices, vending machines, press kiosks and Narvesen shops. A single trip on bus/tram/trolleybus/minibus costs €1.15 (€2 when bought onboard). A five-ride ticket costs €5.75, ten rides are €10.90, and twenty rides are €20.70. Riga Pass comes in several variations (depending on time limit and/or specific interests) and offers unlimited travel on public transport, free sightseeing tours as well as discounts in museums and restaurants. For routes, timetables and fares consult www.rigassatiksme.lv.

Car hire. A compact car with unlimited mileage costs about €30 a day. Sixt (www.sixt.lv) offers all kinds of cars, bicycles and even Vespa scooters (from €35 a day).

Hotels. Accommodation will be your greatest expense in Riga, although rooms can be ridiculously cheap outside of the capital. A bed in a common dormitory in one of the many hostels will start from €15 with a double room in a budget hotel costing at least €40. A mid-range hotel should cost an average of €80. Rates for top-end hotels begin at about €100. Breakfast and twelve percent VAT are almost always included in the price of a room. Room rates can be as much as €20 higher during the short summer season.

Meals and drinks. A main course at a typical restaurant usually costs from around €10. A three-course meal for two in a mid-range restaurant will be around €60. Domestic beer can be bought at a bar for as little as €2. Cocktails can cost more than €5.

Taxis. Make sure to use only licensed taxis with yellow license plates beginning with TX or TE. Always check if the meter is turned on. The maximum day fare is €0.71 per kilometre while the initial fee is €2.15. Two reputable taxi companies are Baltic Taxi (tel: 85 00; http://baltictaxi.com) and Red Cab (tel: 83 83; www.rtp.lv). You can also book taxis from other companies by calling 371 8880.

Entertainment. Tickets to world-class opera and ballet performances, as well as classical music concerts, are relatively cheap, starting from around €10 per ticket. However, the best seats for top performances may cost up to €80.

Guided tours. A proper tour of Riga starts from €15 and day excursions to Sigulda and Rundāle Palace cost from €50.

CAR HIRE

There is no better way to see Latvia's beautiful natural scenery than to hire a car. If limiting your sightseeing to the capital city, hiring a car is not necessary as most of Riga's places of interest can be easily reached on foot, by bicycle or by cheap and efficient public transport. Hiring a car is simple and relatively inexpensive. You must be at least 21 years of age and must possess a valid driving licence (for at least a year), passport and major credit card. Bear in mind that many Latvians are irresponsible drivers who are not above passing on blind turns or suddenly driving in the opposite lane of oncoming traffic to avoid a pothole. Many rural roads, which account for the vast majority of Latvia's infrastructure, are in a sad state of repair. Rental agencies include:

Add Car Rental, Dzirnieku iela 6, Mārupe, tel: 2658 96 74, www.addcar rental.com.

Auto, tel: 2958 04 48, www.carsrent.lv.

Avis Airport, tel: 6720 73 53, www.avis.lv.

Sixt Airport, tel: 6720 71 21, www.sixt.lv.
Budget Rent a Car Airport, tel: 6720 73 27, www.budget.lv.
Europcar Airport, tel: 6720 78 25, www.europcar.lv.
Hertz Airport, tel: 2943 27 69, www.hertz.lv.

> I'd like to hire a car for one day/week **Es vēlos īrēt automašīnu uz dienu/nedēļu**
> Where's the nearest filling station? **Kur ir tuvākā degvielas uzpildes stacija?**
> Full tank, please **Pilnu bāku, lūdzu**

CLIMATE

The best time to visit Riga is during the summer months between mid-May and mid-September. Winters are often wet and harsh with very little sunlight to lift the gloom. It's not uncommon for Riga to experience snow flurries as late as April.

	J	F	M	A	M	J	J	A	S	O	N	D
°C max	-2	-2	3	9	16	19	21	20	15	10	4	0
°C min	-6	-6	-3	2	7	11	13	13	9	5	1	-4
°F max	29	29	37	48	60	66	69	68	59	50	39	32
°F min	22	21	28	35	45	52	56	55	48	41	33	25

CRIME AND SAFETY

Riga is no more dangerous and, in most respects, is safer than many European capitals. Visitors should be most wary of irresponsible drivers and drunken youths in Old Riga after midnight. Organised scams and gangs of pickpockets are nearly unheard of. Avoid the unkempt hawkers of cheap or fake amber and outdated postcards that offer their wares to groups of unsuspecting tourists and foreigners; their goods are rarely the genuine article.

The most common form of petty theft is the snatching of mobile phones at beer gardens, so keep your belongings in your pockets to be on the safe side. Some unlucky expatriates have also been mugged on their way home from bars and clubs in the wee hours of the morning, so a taxi might be a good idea.

I want to report a theft **Es vēlos paziņot par zādzību**

Where is the nearest police station? **Kur ir tuvākais policijas iecirknis?**

Stop thief! **Ķeriet zagli!**

Help! **Palīgā!**

Go away **Ejiet projām**

DRIVING

Much like the rest of the world, a valid driving licence, ID or passport, vehicle registration as well as proof of insurance are required to operate a vehicle in Latvia.

Road conditions. Latvia's roads have steadily improved in recent years but catching up with Western standards might still take some time. Sadly, in terms of fatalities the Latvian roads are among the worst in the EU (see Safety below), which is mainly due to reckless driving habits and difficult weather conditions for most of the year.

Rules and regulations. Like the rest of continental Europe, driving is on the right side of the road. In urban areas and towns, the speed limit is 50kmh (30mph) and 90kmh (55–70mph) on the open road unless marked otherwise. The drink-driving limit is 0.05 percent (equivalent to a half litre of beer) or even 0.02 percent for drivers with less than two years' experience. Speed traps are prevalent. Many Latvian drivers are irresponsible and think nothing of passing when their view is obscured. Driving in the oncoming traffic lane is also quite common, especially if a driver can spare their car's suspension by avoiding potholes. Make sure to have your front lights on at all times and winter tires from December till March.

Safety. Latvia has one of the highest proportions of road-accident casualties in Europe, so it is always best to be hyper-vigilant when driving.

Parking. There are parking meters situated are all over the city. Rates vary according to the zone; the closer you park to Old Riga, the more you pay. Drivers must pay at the meter or by phone (SMS Riga) and place the receipt on the dashboard of their car to avoid it being clamped. Rates can be as high as €10 per hour in the old town. For details visit the website www.rigassatiksme.lv or download its app.

Breakdowns. Should your car experience mechanical problems, call the following toll-free number of the Latvian Automotive Society (LAMB) for 24-hour towing services, tel: 1888, www.lamb.lv.

Gājeji Pedestrians
Stāvvieta Parking
Vienvirziena iela One-way street
Pa kreisi/pa labi Left/right
Bīstami Danger
Apkārtceļš Detour
Stop Stop

ELECTRICITY

The electrical current used in Latvia is 220V AC, 50Hz. Two-pronged European plugs are necessary.

EMBASSIES

Australians and New Zealanders should contact the UK embassy.

Canada Baznīcas 20/22, tel: 6781 39 45, https://www.international.gc.ca.

Republic of Ireland Alberta 13, tel: 6703 93 70, https://www.ireland.ie/en/latvia/riga.

United Kingdom Alunāna 5, tel: 6777 47 00, www.gov.uk/world/organisations/british-embassy-riga.

USA Samnera Velsa 1, tel: 6710 70 00, https://lv.usembassy.gov.

> Where is the British/American Embassy? **Kur ir Lielbritānijas/ Amerikas Vēstniecība?**

EMERGENCIES

In Riga you can dial 112 for any emergency and the operator will connect you to the appropriate authorities.

Fire: 01
Police: 02
Paramedics: 03
Tourist police 24-hour hotline: 6718 18 18
Information hotline: 1188

> Police! **Policija!**
> Fire! **Ugunsgrēks!**
> Help! **Palīgā!**
> Where can I find a doctor who speaks English? **Kur es varu atrast ārstu, kas runā angliski?**

GETTING THERE

By air. The national carrier, airBaltic, www.airbaltic.com, offers affordable direct flights to Riga from London (Gatwick), Brussels, Berlin, Stockholm and several other cities in Europe. The following airlines operate flights to Riga from their local hubs: Norwegian (Oslo), Turkish Airlines (Istanbul), Lufthansa (Frankfurt), Finnair (Helsinki), Aeroflot (Moscow Sheremetevo), and LOT Polish Airlines (Warsaw). Low-cost airlines now offer direct flights to Riga. Ryanair flies from London Stansted, East Midlands, Edinburgh, Leeds Bradford, Manchester and Dublin, while Wizz Air from London (Luton) and Doncaster/Sheffield. If travelling from North America, contact Scandinavian Airlines-SAS, KLM, Lufthansa, Finnair, Czech Airlines, LOT Polish Airlines and Uzbekistan Airways for the most convenient connections to Riga. If travelling from Australia or New Zealand contact KLM or Lufthansa.

By rail. It is possible to reach Latvia by rail from Belarus (Minsk) and Estonia (Valga). For fares and schedules go to www.pv.lv/en.

By road. Eurolines (www.eurolines.lt) runs buses to many European cities, including London. If you're driving your own car, see page 128. Other operators include Ecolines (https://ecolines.net) and Lux Express (www.luxexpress.eu).

GUIDES AND TOURS

Riga Free Tour (https://www.rigafreetours.com) provides regular free guided tours of the capital city, with various focuses including Old Riga; alternative Riga; Soviet history; and Art Nouveau. Check the website for times, meeting places and lengths of tours, and reserve your place online in advance to avoid disappointment. Simple boat tours depart nearly every hour from the Old Riga bank of the River Daugava in the summer and usually cost around €10. Longer boat rides may also include trips to Mežaparks and Jūrmala. Book tickets via https://rivercruises.lv.

Is there an English-speaking guide? **Vai ir pieejams angliski runājošs gīds?**
Can you translate this for me? **Vai jūs varat man šo pārtulkot?**

HEALTH AND MEDICAL CARE

If you're going to spend most of your stay in the Latvian countryside, a vaccination against tick-borne encephalitis is recommended. If, like most visitors, you don't intend on hiking in the hills of Vidzeme or camping in the lake country in Latgale, a vaccination isn't necessary.

A major international health insurance policy, or at least travel insurance, is always recommended, but medication, minor emergency treatments and diagnostic tests are relatively inexpensive in Riga. EU citizens with a valid European Health Insurance Card (EHIC) or UK citizens with a Global Health Insurance Card (GHIC; available from UK post offices or online at https://services.nhsbsa.nhs.uk/cra/start) can receive free emergency treatment. If you feel unwell, your best first stop is a pharmacy – *aptiekas* in Latvian, where you can often find most of what you might need to cure common, temporary ailments. If over-the-counter medicines do not do the trick, it is advisable to seek help from a qualified doctor. Vecpilsētas aptieka, Vaļņu 28 (entrance from Audēju), tel: 2037 74 76, is a 24-hour pharmacy in Old Riga.

The following are reputable emergency-service facilities with English-speaking doctors:

ARS Skolas 5, tel: 6720 10 07, https://arsmed.lv.

Diplomatic Service Medical Centre Elizabetes 57, tel: 6722 99 42, www.dsmc.lv. English-speaking dentists are also among the staff.

Riga Hospital Clinic Bruņinieku 5, tel: 6736 63 23.

LANGUAGE

Latvian is not a Slavic language. Of all of the Indo-European tongues, modern Latvian and Lithuanian are the closest languages to Sanskrit and many words are still remarkably similar to their ancient root words. Latvians are extremely proud of their language and have safeguarded its existence and future use by acts of legislation. Although most Latvians, at least in Riga, still speak Russian, tourists should bear in mind that it is the language of their former occupiers and often not welcomed. Many Latvians over the age of 50 speak German, while the younger generation is often eager to show off its knowledge of English. Any attempt by a foreigner to speak Latvian is often greeted with grateful surprise.

One aspect of the Latvian language is its pursuit to change foreign names and places to fit its grammatical usage. Cities like New York and Munich become Ņujorka and Minhene, while heads of state and film stars become Džordžs Bušs and Breds Pits in Latvian. International news often becomes a confusing display of linguistics, especially when events occur in Africa, Asia and the Middle East.

An easy rule of thumb for foreigners is that an *s*, *is* or *š* is almost always added to the end of male names and an *a* or *e* is added the end of female names. Another peculiarity of the language is that only place names and proper names are capitalised, so the Latvians are *latvieši*, the English are *angļi*, Sunday is *svētdiena* and June is *jūnijs*.

How are you? **Kā jums klājas?/Kā tev iet?**

Pleased to meet you. **Prieks iepazīties.**

Do you speak English? **Vai jūs runājat angliski?**

I don't speak Latvian. **Es nerunāju latviski.**

Where is the nearest hotel/toilet? **Kur atrodas tuvākā viesnīca/tualete?**

What's your name? **Kā jūs/tevi sauc?**

My name is ... **Mani sauc ...**

What time is it? **Cik ir pulkstenis?**

LGBTQ+ TRAVELLERS

Although some of Latvia's most prominent journalists, patrons of the arts and restaurateurs are openly gay, acceptance by the general public has still not been forthcoming. LGBTQ+ travellers should expect stares or perhaps giggles for public displays of affection as benign as holding hands. While there is no specific gay quarter is Riga, most of the action can be found in *Top Club* and a few gay saunas around Alfrēda Kalniņa iela. For information on gay nightlife visit https://topclub.lv or www.mygoldenclub.com/en/contact. Baltic Pride is hosted in turn by Estonia, Lithuania, and Latvia, with Riga next taking the reins in 2027; check https://www.facebook.com/BalticPride for details. For useful LGBTQ+ resources, including information on health, events and LGBTQ+ rights, or to find out about the history of the queer community in Latvia, visit www.mozaika.lv.

MONEY

In 2014 Latvia replaced the lat (Ls) with the euro. Notes are issued in denominations of 5, 10, 20, 50, 100, 200 and 500 euros. Coins in circulation are 1, 2, 5, 10, 20 and 50 centimos and 1 and 2 euros.

Currency exchange. Currency exchanges, some open 24 hours, are widely available, especially in Old Riga. Rates vary and tend to be poorest in the touristy areas and in banks. You should always check the rates before exchanging any money, but scams and widely differing rates are rare in Riga.

Do you accept credit cards? **Vai varu maksāt ar kredītkarti?**
How much is this? **Cik tas maksā?**
I want to change some pounds/dollars into lats **Es vēlos apmainīt dažus mārciņas/dolārus latos**
Where's the nearest bank/currency exchange office? **Kur ir tuvākā banka/naudas apmaiņas birojs?**
What's the exchange rate? **Kāds ir maiņas kurss?**

Credit cards. Credit cards are used nearly as much as, if not more than, cash. Most hotels, restaurants, many shops and even taxis accept major international credit and debit cards.

ATMs. Cash machines or ATMs, known locally as *bankomāti*, are located on nearly every street corner in Old Riga and the city centre and accept all major credit and debit cards.

OPENING TIMES

With the exception of major shopping centres, which are usually open daily 10am–10pm, most shops are open 9am–5pm, shorter on weekends. Banks and government offices are generally open weekdays 9am–5pm. Most museums are open 10am–6pm (close earlier in winter) and many are closed on Mondays and even Tuesdays. Typical office hours are 9am–5pm Monday to Friday.

POLICE

The Latvian police force has been modernised, but stories of corruption and unprofessionalism are still not uncommon. Emergency services operators have been known to hang up on callers and a general air of apathy seems to pervade the police force. Thankfully, or not depending on your point of view, most traffic police no longer take bribes, but foreign visitors have been scooped up at various locations throughout the city for being, what the law enforcers deem, inebriated. Avoid a trip to the drunk tank at all costs. These, for the most part, are isolated incidences so you should not hesitate to contact the police if in trouble. During the summer months, police stroll the old city in great numbers making sure that tourists don't become the victims of pickpockets or muggers.

Where's the nearest police station? **Kur ir tuvākais policijas iecirknis?**

I've lost my wallet/handbag/passport **Es esmu pazaudējis savu naudas maku/rokas somu/pasi**

PUBLIC HOLIDAYS

Banks and government offices are closed on the following holidays:

1 January **New Year's Day** *Jaungads*

March/April **Good Friday** *Lielā piektdiena*

March/April **Easter Sunday** *Lieldienas*

March/April **Easter Monday** *Otrās Lieldienas*

1 May **Labour Day** *Strādnieku diena*

4 May **Proclamation of Independence (1990)** *Valsts svētki*

23–24 June **Midsummer** *Līgo & Jāņi*

18 November **Independence Day (1918)** *Valsts svētki*

24–26 December **Christmas** *Ziemassvētki*

31 December **New Year's Eve** *Vecgada vakars*

PUBLIC TRANSPORT

All public transport in Rīga, including trams, buses, and trolleybuses, runs from around 5am to 11pm, after which night buses come into operation. E-tickets (cards) can be acquired at vending machines, Narvesen kiosks, Rimi supermarkets and a number of other outlets. Money loaded onto the e-ticket to cover one (€1.50), two (€3.00), 10 (€15) rides or tickets for unlimited one-day (€5), three-day (€8) or five-day (€10) travel. Alternatively, "code tickets" can be bought and downloaded onto your mobile phone via the Rīgas Satiksme app. Always make sure to validate your ticket against the electronic reader as soon as you board the bus, tram or trolley. For more information in English, visit the Tram and Trolleybus Authority's site, www. rigassatiksme.lv. Minibuses called *mikroautobusi*, or *mikriņi* for short, can also be a convenient way of travelling, as they will stop at any point along a given route. But they are slightly more expensive and make frequent stops to pick up more passengers when the small van is already packed like a tin of sardines.

Trams. Electric trams have been in use in Riga since 1901. Today, there are eight different tramlines, numbered 1, 2, 3, 5, 7, 9, 10 and 11, which together cover 182km (113 miles) of Riga. More than 270 trams service a total of over 33 million passengers each year. Trams operate from 5am to midnight, and night trams are in service approximately every hour on weekend nights.

Trolleybuses. There are seventeen different trolleybuses one can take to destinations near and far. The same rules for trams apply to trolleybuses.

How much is the fare to...? **Cik maksā biļete līdz...?**
I want a ticket to ... single (one-way)/return (round-trip) **Es vēlos biļeti vienā virzienā/turp un atpakaļ**
How long does the journey take? **Cik ilgi ir jābrauc?**
Will you tell me when to get off? **Lūdzu pasakiet, kad jaizkāpj?**

Taxis. Respectable firms should charge no more than €2.15 for pick up, €0.71 (daytime) per kilometre. Always insist on the meter being turned on or agree on a price beforehand. Smile Taxi (tel: 0330, www.smiletaxi.lv), Red Cab Taxi (tel: 8383, http://redcab.lv) and Baltic Taxi (http://baltictaxi.com) are all respected taxi firms. Alternatively, download the Bolt app (www.

bolt.eu). Uber is not currently present in Latvia. You can also wave down taxis on any street, but to avoid exorbitant prices it's best to always call a cab or ask the receptionist at your hotel to order a taxi for you.

Note that all official taxis must display a yellow number plate. Taxis at the train and bus stations are notoriously dishonest, but cabs at the airport are reputable.

> How much is it to...? **Cik maksā līdz...?**
> Take me to this address **Lūdzu brauciet uz šo adresi**
> Please stop here. **Lūdzu apstājieties šeit.**

TELEPHONES

To call Latvia from abroad, dial your country's international dialling code (00 within Europe) and Latvia's country code (371), followed by the number, minus the first (0) of the area code. To call abroad from Latvia dial 00, the country code, and then the number, minus the first (0) of the area code.
Public phones. Public phones are still available in some places across the city, but a phone card is required to operate them. Cards can be bought at most kiosks and shops which display the *telekarte* sign. You can also use a credit card to make a call from a phone booth – just follow the instructions.
Mobile phones. Smartphones will automatically switch over to a local service once you arrive. Citizens of EU and European Economic Area (EEA) countries do not pay temporary roaming charges in Latvia. UK operators have different policies on roaming in the EU and you should check your contract before travelling. To avoid roaming charges altogether, you can get a local number by buying an inexpensive starter kit, sold in kiosks and shops, which comes with prepaid credit. Latvian mobile numbers have eight digits, starting with 2.

TICKETS

Tickets for world-class performances of the opera and ballet, as well as classical concerts, are usually only available at the venue's box-office, but are almost always relatively affordable. Tickets for international pop music concerts and other large events on the other hand are often expensive by local standards. Tickets for these events can usually be purchased at the information desk at the railway station and at the customer service desk at Stockmann, 13 janvāra 8.

TIME ZONES

Latvia is in the Eastern European Time zone, which is GMT +2 hours. An hour is added between the end of March and October for daylight savings, so during the summer local time is GMT +3 hours, known as Eastern European Summer Time or EEST for short.

New York	London	**Riga**	Jo'burg	Sydney	Auckland
6am	11am	**1pm**	1pm	10pm	midnight

TIPPING

Service is not included in most bills. Round up the sum of the bill and add a little if service was appreciated. No more than ten percent is expected.

TOILETS

Many public toilets throughout the city are in a sad state. The only exceptions are the toilets at the train station and on Līvu Square, but restaurants, cafés and hotel lobbies are still your best option. Men's and women's toilets are usually designated with a triangle pointing down or up, respectively.

Where are the toilets? **Kur ir tualetes?**

TOURIST INFORMATION

Although limited information can be gleaned from a variety of unofficial sources at the airport and at bus and train stations, the best place to find tourist information is the Riga Information Centre, Rātslaukums 6, tel: 6703

79 00, www.liveriga.com. For a full list of Latvian information centres visit www.latvia.travel. For maps and information about restaurants, nightlife, museums and local events pick up a copy of the excellent *Riga In Your Pocket* city guide, which is published once every two months. City maps are readily available at the Rīga Information Centre, or alternatively you can find a large selection of inexpensive maps and guides of Latvia and the Baltic region at the excellent Jāņa Sēta Map Shop, Elizabetes 83/85; www.mapshop.lv.

VISAS AND ENTRY REQUIREMENTS

Passports/Visas. All citizens of the EU, US, United Kingdom, as well as Canadians, Australians and New Zealanders only need a valid passport to enter Latvia and can stay up to ninety days every six months without a visa. Citizens of South Africa need a visa to visit Latvia.

Vaccinations. You do not need any special vaccinations to enter Latvia, but cases of tick-borne encephalitis are not uncommon in the countryside. People are advised to check themselves for ticks – tiny black mites in the skin – after tramping through tall brush.

Customs. Individuals entering and leaving Latvia may carry with them most articles, personal property and other valuables in unlimited quantities. However, weapons and ammunition of any kind, drugs and psychotropic substances are not allowed. Restrictions on alcohol and cigarettes/cigars also apply. There are no limits on the amount of currency you may bring with you to Latvia. Amounts exceeding €10,000 should be declared when arriving from a non-EU country.

YOUR TAILOR-MADE TRIP
STARTS HERE

Tailor-made trips and unique adventures crafted by local experts

Rough Guides has been inspiring travellers with lively an thought-provoking guidebooks for more than 35 years. Now we're linking you up with selected local experts to craft your dream trip. They will put together your perfec itinerary and book it at local rates.

Don't follow the crowd – find your own path.

HOW ROUGHGUIDES.COM/TRIPS WORKS

STEP 1

Pick your dream destination, tell us what you want and submit an enquiry.

STEP 2

Fill in a short form to tell your local expert about yo dream trip and preference

STEP 3

Our local expert will craft your tailor-made itinerary. You'll be able to tweak and refine it until you're completely satisfied.

STEP 4

Book online with ease, pa your bags and enjoy the trip! Our local expert will b on hand 24/7 while you're on the road.

BENEFITS OF PLANNING AND BOOKING AT
ROUGHGUIDES.COM/TRIPS

LAN YOUR ADVENTURE WITH LOCAL EXPERTS

Rough Guides' English-speaking local experts are hand-picked, based n their experience in the ravel industry and their npeccable standards of customer service.

SAVE TIME AND GET ACCESS TO LOCAL KNOWLEDGE

When a local expert plans your trip, you save time and money when you book, even during high season. You won't be charged for using a credit card either.

MAKE TRAVEL A BREEZE: BOOK WITH PEACE OF MIND

Enjoy stress-free travel when you use Rough Guides' secure online booking platform. All bookings come with a money-back guarantee.

WHAT DO OTHER TRAVELLERS THINK
ABOUT ROUGH GUIDES TRIPS?

rip to Spain

This Spain tour company did a fantastic job to make our dream trip perfect. We gave them our travel budget, told them where we would like to go, and they did all of the planning. Our drivers and tour guides were always on time and very knowledgable. The hotel accommodations were better than we would have found on our own. Only one time did we end up in a location that we had not intended to be in. We called the 24 hour phone number, and they immediately fixed the situation.

Don A, USA ★★★★★

LAN AND BOOK YOUR TRIP AT
OUGHGUIDES.COM/TRIPS

THE **MINI** ROUGH GUIDE TO
RIGA

First edition 2025

Editor: Joanna Reeves
Author: Martins Zaprauskis
Updater: Joanna Reeves
Picture Editor: Piotr Kala
Picture Manager: Tom Smyth
Cartography Update: Katie Bennett
Layout: Grzegorz Madejak
Production Operations Manager: Katie Bennett
Publishing Technology Manager: Rebeka Davies
Head of Publishing: Sarah Clark
Photography Credits: All images Shutterstock
except: iStock 12BL, 12TR, 12BR, 12CR, 36, 40, 43,
53, 54, 61, 73, 85, 86, 99; Melnie Mūki 14T; Micah
Sarut/Apa Publications 7, 12BC, 14CL, 30, 81, 83,
89, 95, 111, 115; Public domain 21, 25, 26, 29;
Reinis Hofmanis/Investment and Development
Agency of Latvia 13B; Ģirts Raģelis/Investment
and Development Agency of Latvia 45
Cover Credits: Schwabe House And House
Of The Blackheads **George Trumpeter/
Shutterstock**

About the author

Joanna Reeves is a Sussex-based travel writer and
editor who has updated several Rough Guides,
including parts of the Rough Guides to England
and Great Britain, Pocket Rough Guide Reykjavik
and the Rough Guide Mini Bologna. She is also
the editor of the brand-new Rough Guide to
Slow Travel in Europe.

Distribution

UK, Ireland and Europe: Apa Publications (UK)
Ltd; sales@roughguides.com
United States and Canada: Ingram Publisher
Services; ips@ingramcontent.com

Australia and New Zealand: Booktopia;
retailer@booktopia.com.au
Worldwide: Apa Publications (UK) Ltd;
sales@roughguides.com

Special Sales, Content Licensing and CoPublishing

Rough Guides can be purchased in bulk
quantities at discounted prices. We can create
special editions, personalised jackets and
corporate imprints tailored to your needs.
sales@roughguides.com; http://roughguides.com

Contact us

Every effort has been made to provide accurate
information in this publication, but changes
are inevitable. The publisher cannot be held
responsible for any resulting loss, inconvenience
or injury sustained by any traveller as a result
of information or advice contained in the
guide. We would appreciate it if readers would
call our attention to any errors or outdated
information, or if you feel we've left something
out. Please send your comments with the
subject line "Rough Guide Mini Riga Update" to
mail@uk.roughguides.com.